BLOWING OFF STEAM

BLOWING OFF STEAM

Tales of an LMS fireman, 1941-54

Jack Backen

Silver Link Publishing Ltd

To Nan,
with lots of love and thanks for her support
and understanding. . .always

ACKNOWLEDGEMENTS

The author would like to acknowledge the kind help and advice of the following:

The Nottingham Evening Post for kind permission to reproduce photographs; Mac Johnstone for the generous loan of his photographic collection, some of which appears in this book; Barbara Binch, Joyce Skinner and Noel Limb, who kindly agreed to type the work; and Steve Sands, who helped out just a little whenever he could.

And especially to my wife, Maisie, without whose help and understanding this work would never have been completed.

First published in September 1993
Reprinted July 1995

British Library Cataloguing in Publication Data

A catalogue record for this book is available from the British Library

ISBN 1 85794 003 2

To avoid any possible embarrassment to the people concerned, certain of the names and locations mentioned in this book have been changed.

Silver Link Publishing Ltd
Unit 5
Home Farm Close
Church Street
Wadenhoe
Peterborough
PE8 5TE
Tel/fax (01832) 720440

Map drawn by Christina Siviter

Printed and bound in Great Britain

CONTENTS

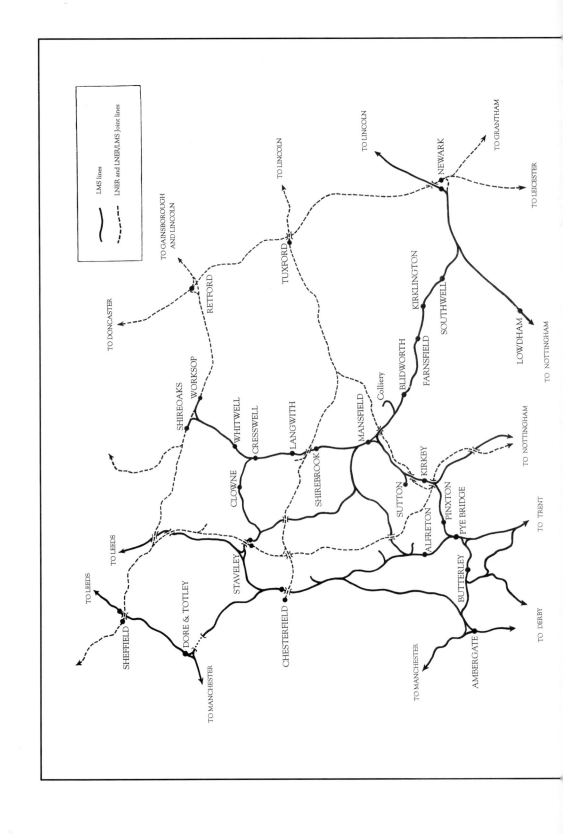

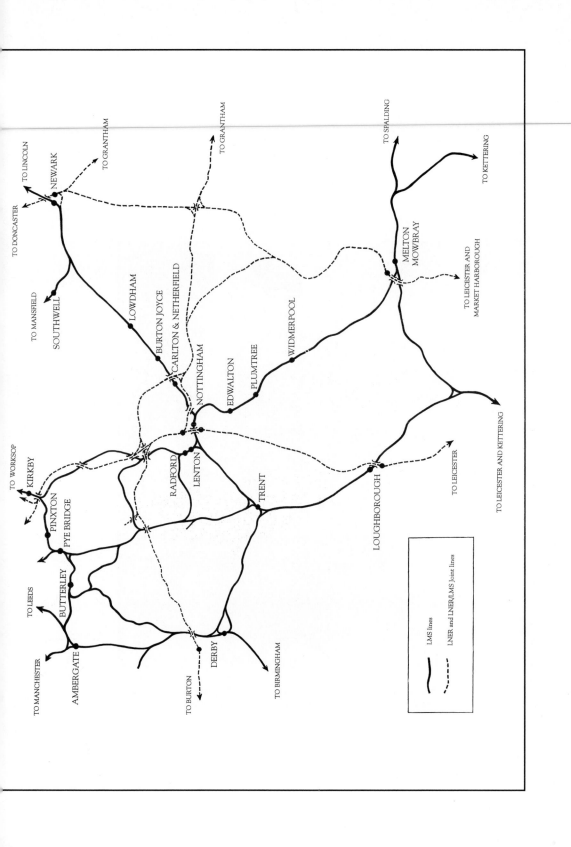

TO LINCOLN

TO DONCASTER

TO GRANTHAM

TO GRANTHAM

TO SPALDING

TO KETTERING

NEWARK

TO MANSFIELD

SOUTHWELL

LOWDHAM

BURTON JOYCE

CARLTON & NETHERFIELD

MELTON
MOWBRAY

TO LEICESTER AND
MARKET HARBOROUGH

NOTTINGHAM

EDWALTON

PLUMTREE

WIDMERPOOL

TO WORKSOP

KIRKBY

PINXTON

PYE BRIDGE

RADFORD

LENTON

TRENT

LOUGHBOROUGH

TO LEICESTER

TO LEICESTER AND KETTERING

TO LEEDS

BUTTERLEY

TO MANCHESTER

AMBERGATE

DERBY

TO BURTON

TO BIRMINGHAM

LMS lines

LNER and LNER/LMS joint lines

'The first of the line. . .' My grandfather, John Bagshaw Backen, resplendent in the uniform of a passenger guard, *circa* 1910. *Author*

INTRODUCTION

I was five years old when my father first introduced me to the never-to-be-forgotten mixture of smoke, oil and steam that I met when I walked into the locomotive and engine shed. What a terrifying yet magnetic experience that was! I have remembered it all my life.

The sight and sound of those tremendous steel monsters that were railway engines captivated me, yet at the same time filled me with terror. The hiss of steam from safety valves and columns of smoke from chimneys, the smell of hot oil, smoke and steam convinced me of my future life. I wanted to be a part of this awesome power. I wanted to be on the footplate!

In those early days that now seem so long ago the highlights of my life were the Sunday afternoon shifts when my father was on duty and the only man in the 'Loco' - Kirkby locomotive engine shed, Kirkby-in-Ashfield, Nottinghamshire - for then off we would go on his bicycle to the depot five miles distant. My mother would have already packed my 'snap', one jam buttie and a piece of cake in my little snap tin, not forgetting, of course, a 'mashing' of tea just like dad's. What a great adventure it all was.

My father was what was then called a 'steam-raiser'. His job was to light the fires in the engines to get the boilers up to steam pressure ready for work on the following day. The drivers and firemen would be signing on from midnight. In those days the day shift would sign on at all hours between one minute past midnight and one minute to midday, when the afternoon shift would take over and relieve them. On the notice-board in the shed would be all the engine numbers and the destinations for which they would be bound. For example, there would be '8394 at 12.01 for Wellingborough', '8112 at 12.25 for Manchester', and so on. All these numbers and destinations used to bewilder me.

On shift my father would have 70 to 90 engines in his charge, but having had ten years experience the job was comparatively easy to him. Once some of the engines left the loco shed they might not be seen again for a week or more, depending on where they were bound. The crews would be relieved by other crews and the great pounding engines would haul north, east, south or west, calling in at other loco sheds, up-line or down-line, to have their fires cleaned and take on fresh supplies of coal and water for other runs before eventually arriving back at their home base.

For me, those hours on the Sunday went far too quickly. I would be up and down on the footplates from two o'clock until six with my very own little firing shovel stoking away with dad. And then it was 'snap' time when we would brew up by putting a billy-can of water on the lip of a firebox and within five minutes it would be boiling. What a thrill it was to sit there on the driver's seat, covered all over with soot and grime and smoke and oil eating our sandwiches and drinking our tea. What a marvellous way to spend a Sunday afternoon. I wouldn't have changed places with the King!

One of the highlights of those Sunday afternoons was when some of the drivers and firemen would bring their wives and girlfriends to have a look at the engines - a great

Left My father was P. T. ('Darky') Backen. Here he is with the 1st Lincolns just landed in France in 1914 - he is second from the right, back row. *Author*

Below left Ready for action, 1914. 'Darky' is in front at the left with a Lee Enfield rifle. *Author*

privilege denied most ordinary mortals. Dad, having spotted them, would send me off with a clean white duster so that they could keep their hands clean, and for which I would sometimes receive a penny, or sometimes a whole sixpence, and then it would be off across the road to the sweet-shop. If I had had a successful day with the white duster trade it would be a packet of Woodbines for dad, a twopenny bar of Bournville for mam and enough sweets to last me the whole of the week at school. I was the envy of all my school pals. To be allowed on the footplate of a real engine and get free sweets into the bargain was more than any normal person could possibly hope for.

Without a doubt the most thrilling memory of those happy Sundays, and as far as my school pals were concerned the final *pièce de résistance*, was the time my father decided I was actually old enough to have a ride on one of those magnificent engines. When he told me what we were about to do I was thrilled and terrified at the same time, but then, at five years old, I thought there was little to lose. I mean, at that age you've seen it all and done it all, so I decided 'This is it,

My father as a prisoner of war somewhere in Germany, 1918. *Author*
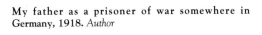

Above My parents, 'Darky' and Marie Backen, on holiday in Southsea in the late 'forties. *Author*

Above right The author aged 2, before he started blowing off steam. . . *Author*

Right My father and father-in-law, Harold William Gosling, off to the races in 1975. *Author*

it's muck or nettles now. If we go down we will go down with flags flying.'

After all, I couldn't be in better company. Hadn't my dad fought the whole German army and, according to him, killed most of them single-handed? He always used to tell me he killed at least three before breakfast. I must admit that the way he used to tell me how he killed them put me off my breakfast most mornings.

But to get back to that never-to-be-forgotten day, we climbed on to the footplate of No 8112, one of the finest engines on the LMS, a Class '8' freight locomotive capable of pulling 80 wagons of coal from Kirkby to Brent, near London, non-stop, picking up water from troughs with its scoop *en route*.

She was pointing chimney-first out of the shed with about half a mile of track to run on before we reached the limit of the loco-yard where there was a signal and a set of 'jack

Above LMS 2-8-0 Class '8F' No 8094, similar to the loco that gave me my first taste of the footplate, seen here at Crewe in August 1938. *G. A. Barlow, Mac Johnstone collection*

Left A snap of 'Darky' Backen (right) on the running-plate of '8F' 2-8-0 No 48006 at Kirkby on Sunday afternoon, 10 May 1953. *Author*

points' that would de-rail you if you ran past; we therefore had just enough room to manoeuvre, although with an engine 30 yards long and weighing 120 tons you needed every yard possible.

We looked at the steam pressure gauge and found we had 150 pounds per square inch, giving us plenty of steam to play with. We applied the steam brake and were thus able to release the hand brake. We then spun the reversing lever into forward gear, closed the cylinder taps, opened the regulator, and, with a blast on the whistle and a tremendous hiss of steam and vibra-

tion of power, slowly pulled away.

Dad had sat me on the fireman's seat where I was hanging on for dear life. I could just see over the edge of the window and we were now puffing up the yard. I imagined we were the 'Royal Scot' doing a hundred miles an hour instead of just shunting along at little more than walking pace. Still, I thought at five years old that they wouldn't let me fire the 'Royal Scot' yet, so this was the next best thing.

Dad switched the points that took us on to the turntable where he connected the vacuum pipes and turned the engine round for our return run into the Loco, where we buffered up to another Class '8' with a loud clang. Boy, what a thrill!

At the end of the day I was practically asleep on dad's crossbar as we made our way home. When I walked in, black and smelly but happy, my mother took one look at me and started getting on to dad for bringing me home in such a state. Then, for me, the most unpleasant part of the day arrived.

'Come on, into the bath, and don't you dare get out until you're white again!' said my mother.

Dad gave me a wink saying, 'I can't imagine how he got so black, but hurry up so's we can have some supper.'

This pacified mum, for she was only making a pretence at being cross, and in no time at all I changed colour and was back downstairs where I ate about three suppers before being packed off to bed. It seemed as though I would sleep for a week.

When I eventually woke up the first

Right '8F' 2-8-0 No 48460 standing in the yard at Kirkby Loco in August 1955. *Derek Murdoch*

Below '8F' No 48006 again, taking centre stage in this panorama of Kirkby depot taken almost five years after the picture opposite, in March 1958. Note the new ashpits being constructed on the right. *K. C. H. Fairey*

thought that came into my head was that I would have to wait three more weeks before I could have another day out with dad on the Loco. I used to look forward to those Sundays all through my school years, but I must admit that when I was approaching thirteen or fourteen years of age other priorities temporarily pushed them out of my mind. Things like going out with my mates.

And girls.

Another of the trusty '8Fs', No 48098, on shed at Kirkby, standing in front of the coaling plant. Note the small tipper wagons beside the engine - these were used to carry away the ashes. The photograph was taken towards the end of steam on BR, 1 November 1965. *K. C. H. Fairey*

1
FIRST RUNG ON THE LADDER

On a certain morning in January 1941, I found myself in the office of the Superintendent of Mansfield Motive Power Depot, a gentleman by the name of Mr Barnacle. This was a name I was to remember all too well in the months and years that lay ahead. I was accompanied into the office by Alan Penford. We had become very good friends over the previous three years when we had both been employed as butchers. It was a job we both heartily disliked but due to the rules and regulations that existed then you had to have a job to go to or you were not allowed to leave school, so we took the first opportunity that came our way. Anything to get away from school, which we both hated.

We were given an eye test on that first railway day, the significance of which was to make itself more apparent to me as the years went by, and the importance of which could

not be overstated. The safety, the very lives, of the people for whom you were responsible often depended on having very keen eyesight. We were both immediately offered an opportunity to become engine cleaners. We both gratefully accepted. At least we had our feet on the first rungs of the ladder, and we were to start on the following Monday.

During the next three days, before we actually started on our new career, Alan was forced into a decision that was to prove most tragic for him. His father did not see his future life as a railwayman being either rewarding or secure enough for him, and strongly advised him to have second thoughts on his impulsive and immature ideas. Alan had no option but to take his father's 'advice' and wrote a letter to Mr Barnacle explaining his reasons for his non-appearance on the following Monday. So I

'Oh, to be a butcher's boy.' Myself and my sister Lois in about 1939. *Author*

started my new life on my own. Alan, being guided by his father, went into the hosiery trade.

When the war started in 1939, Alan and I, who still remained firm friends, had no thought of the terrible tragedy that was later to unfold. When we were both 18^1/$_2$ we received our call-up papers, as did everyone else around that age. Together we went down to the Army Drill Hall in Mansfield for our medical and aptitude tests. We both passed A1 and Alan chose to go into the Royal Marines whilst I chose the Navy. All this took approximately two hours, but everything depended on the answer to the last question.

'What is your present occupation?'

My job on the railway was classed as a 'reserved occupation', whilst Alan's, in the hosiery trade, was not.

During the following year after he was called up, Alan always made a point of seeing me whenever he was home on leave and I often used to admire him in his smart uniform with his red peaked cap.

At last the great day had arrived - 18 January 1941. I was then eighteen years of age and able to follow in my father's footsteps and those of his father before him. I could at last join the London Midland & Scottish Railway.

At eight o'clock sharp on the Monday morning I presented myself for work at the locomotive depot. My duties entailed joining forces with other cleaners in gangs of four. After being issued with bundles of cloths and buckets of what was known as lush, an obnoxious mixture of paraffin, oil and other unmentionable ingredients, our task for the day consisted of washing down with said mixture four engines which were in the Loco for various repairs, then polishing them with the cloths until you could see your face reflected in them. Woe betide the cleaners if the engines did not shine like new pins when Mr Barnacle came to inspect them.

An ignoble beginning, you might think, for the start of our careers as future drivers and firemen on the great LMS Railway, but it was one of the very strict rules of the railway,

amongst many others, that whatever the grade of work in which you first started you would remain in it for the rest of your working life. For instance, if you started as a porter, or a platelayer, or a guard, then this would be your duty in the future.

I was indeed fortunate in being able to draw on my father's advice as to which grade I needed to start in for my life on the footplate, and, strange as it seemed at the time, this was it. An engine cleaner. I was to be grateful many times over for this wise guidance, for there was only ever one good job on the railway, and that was on the footplate. The pay was much better, and once you took your engine off the Loco you were, to a great extent, your own boss.

All this, though, lay in the future, and our present task as cleaners at the time was to make sure that all the engines were spick and span, outside and inside, because Mr Barnacle's beady eyes never missed a thing. The footplate itself came in for very special attention. All the controls, which were made of solid brass, had to be burnished until they shone like a mirror; this in itself took at least two hours of solid rubbing. All this hard work for six days a week for the princely sum of two pounds.

The reason for all this detail was that these were still, in spirit, the railways of the momentous years of the 'twenties and 'thirties, where great rivalry existed between the four main companies, namely the LMS, LNER, SR and GWR. The companies would vie with one another and cut minutes off journeys of a hundred or more miles, and pennies per ton off coal and freight, so you can well imagine the tremendous burden of responsibility that was put on the shoulders of the train drivers. To be able to cope with this intense competition, the engines, rolling-stock and track had to be maintained to a standard of the highest possible order. Also the drivers and firemen who manned these trains were used to strict disciplines and capable of making instant decisions; these were the main reasons why the railways of Great Britain were the envy of the rest of the world.

Many of the drivers of passenger trains had

Mansfield Loco, 10 July 1955. *K. C. H. Fairey*

their own engines with their name written on the side of the cab, and the first thing each would do when he came on duty was to draw a white duster from the stores and wipe all around the controls on the footplate. If the cloth picked up any dirt or grease he would refuse to take his engine off the Loco until things had been repolished, and, again, woe betide the cleaners responsible.

As is often the case, this type of environment bred interesting and unusual characters, many of whom I was to become involved with in the future.

One of the characters we came into contact with during our engine cleaning period in the Loco was a craftsman by the name of Billy Blinkhorn, nick-named 'Bill the Brick'. He possessed a narrow pinched face, and whatever teeth God had blessed him with on being hatched had dropped out long since. His toothlessness gave the effect of his cheeks touching in the middle, causing his beaky little nose to almost touch his chin. A pair of bird-like darting eyes could spot anyone that remotely suggested authority a mile off, and his Adam's-apple would nip up and down his scrawny little throat like a jack-rabbit whenever he excitedly attempted to make a point.

The nickname he had acquired was due to the nature of his job - he built the brick arches in the engine fireboxes. A very important job this, for the purpose of the brick arch was to deflect the intense heat generated by the fire and disperse it around the perimeter of the boiler before allowing it to escape through the tubes and be exhausted into the atmosphere.

Billy was a 'one-off'. They threw the mould away after casting him. I've never met his like before, or since. We, as young cleaners, always imagined him to be black by birth, for this was the only colour that ever materialised as he loomed out of the darkness dressed in his blacker-than-black boiler-suit and cap. He never bought any snap or mashings of tea, preferring instead to beg, borrow or steal anything he could off anybody. So, between us, we used to make him up a 'cocktail'. Any sandwiches we had left over would do, usually cheese, jam, Marmite or marmalade, with a sprinkling of coal dust for added taste. His beverages consisted of tea, coffee and cocoa plus a generous helping of the dreaded lush, our engine cleaning concoction, to make it seem more palatable. Naturally they were all mixed together. He seemed to thrive on it.

After having partaken of his meal he would disappear into one of the fireboxes of an engine in for repair, armed with his fire-bricks and fire-clay. Once he was firmly ensconced after wriggling through the firebox doors and firmly sitting upon his little wooden box strategically placed on the firebars, we would close the doors on him and light an oily rag, tossing it underneath him in the damper. This had no effect whatever. I can only assume the reason was that, to him, it was reminiscent of the noxious substances he was used to smoking in his roll-ups. Dried leaves and privet seemed to be his favourite, plus his very own home-grown tobacco which he used to cure with black treacle. His lungs must have been the same colour as his face!

His tobacco patch in the garden where he lived on Bradder Street, only a stone's throw from the Loco, he jealously guarded. You were never allowed to catch a glimpse of it. It was surrounded by a high fence and covered over by what appeared to be one of his wife's old discarded nighties. Bright scarlet to scare the birds away, I imagined. But they needn't have bothered. If the birds had taken even the slightest peck at his precious tobacco plants I'm certain they would have flipped over on to their backs and turned up their toes to high heaven. We could only guess at the nature of those plants, never having been allowed the privilege of seeing them. Pot, heroin, cannabis, Indian hemp, take your pick. But tobacco? Never in this world.

After completing his stint in the firebox and levering the doors open with a chisel, which provided him with a means of escape, he would glide along the shadows of the Loco in order to avoid the beady eyes of the night foreman and disappear over the top of the 12-foot-high sand-pit for his siesta on the warm sand.

There were two fires built into the bottom of the sand-pit and tending them was one of the jobs we cleaners were delegated to do. We had to keep them just alight and simmer-ing to dry out the sand, which the registered firemen would collect to top up the sand-boxes on any engine that it was their job to repair. Naturally, as soon as Old Bill had gone firmly off to sleep (evidence of this was the sound of snoring loud enough to wake the night foreman in his office 200 yards away had he too not been asleep), we would prodigiously stoke up the fires to such an extent that steam would soon be rising out of the sand like a San Francisco fog. Bill absolutely revelled in it. I believe they call it a Turkish bath or a sauna.

There was no way the foreman would have found him anyway. We had completely covered him in steaming sand, leaving him just a tiny nose-hole to breathe through. Well, we reasoned, we wouldn't want Old Bill to be asphyxiated completely. One of us would have to do his job, and a rotten job it was too! So whilst we wanted to warm Bill up a bit, we did not want him to expire.

The following morning, at knocking-off time, Old Bill would rise like a ministering angel out of his warm bed, stretch himself and, with the look on his face of a man who has just spent the night in the arms of Morpheus, climb elegantly down the ladder, saunter into the office, demand his signing-off card and stagger home to the arms of his wife as though he had been carrying the world on his shoulders for the last eight hours. Yes, a truly happy man.

But talking about his wife - what a contrast! Whilst Bill was about four foot nothing and weighed around seven stone wet through, his wife, better known as 'Big Bessy' by one and all at the Loco, was six foot if she was an inch and must have been six feet around the middle as she weighed all of eighteen stone. This could have been the reason for the look of pure delight on Bill's face when he awakened from his slumber - he could have dreaming about 'Big Bessy'. Wrapped in the arms of Morpheus indeed!

Despite our efforts to keep Bill alive and kicking, one day we nearly lost him when he came within a whisker of floating through the Pearly Gates on a giant cloud of oily smoke. One of his other favourite spots to enjoy a nightly siesta was in the firebox of a dead engine, all the more so if it happened to be still warm.

On this occasion one of the cleaners, Charley Pye, had been instructed to fire up Class '4' No 3997 ready for the next day's work. After arming himself with fire-lighters and oily rags, he opened the firebox doors, lit the rags on the shovel and threw them inside. He was just about to follow them with the fire-lighters when there was an almighty scream.

'What the bloody hell's goin' off? Let me out! Help! Let me out!'

Poor old Charley staggered back, dropping his shovel with a clang.

'That's funny,' he muttered. 'Didn't know this engine could talk - she's never spoke to me before.'

But it wasn't 3997 yelling at Charley, it was Bill the Brick. He poked his head out, coughing and spluttering, cap on one side and a fag hanging from the corner of his mouth.

'What the bloody hell do you think you're doing?' he spat at Charley. 'I'm not dead yet - you're not supposed to cremate people 'til they've been certified!'

In our opinion Bill should have been certified years ago. He crawled rapidly through the doors on to the footplate, his clothes smouldering. There's not much doubt that if he'd stayed in there much longer in his oily-rag boiler-suit he would have gone off like an atom bomb.

He climbed down the steps and scurried off into the sand-hole muttering something to himself about 'A bloke can't even get a good night's kip without some daft bugger trying to set fire to him.'

Needless to say, Old Bill never dropped off in a firebox again. 'They're not using me as a bloody fire-lighter,' he would grumble. 'Don't know what my Bessy would do without me.'

But there were two Bills - not just the one we knew at work, filthy, scruffy, and unkempt, but another Bill. A William, as Big Bessy would address him. And growing his obnoxious smoking material wasn't his only hobby, we discovered. He had another one, a much more refined, and profitable, one. He

Walt Haynes filling up a Class '3' passenger tank engine with water for the return journey. *Walter Haynes*

bred and trained Pomeranian dogs.

By the look of him and his dogs, we imagined for a wild moment that he also fathered them. But no, we reflected - even Old Bill wasn't capable of that! The dogs looked far too refined and well bred to have had a dad like Bill. This revelation could have remained undiscovered for time immemorial if it hadn't have been for a chance meeting one Friday morning when we cleaners were on our way from the Loco down to Mansfield station to receive our weekly fortune. By gum, what a truly marvellous day was pay day. For a few brief hours we would be rich.

We were larking about, as all carefree young men the world over do, when on this particular day who should be strolling towards us but this very elegant large lady dressed in furs and a beautiful pink chiffon hat complete with veil. By her side was a diminutive figure of a man attired in black morning suit, black Homburg hat, highly polished boots, and white spats all admirably complimented by a cravat, smart grey gloves and a large red rose in his button-hole. They were being preceded by eight beautifully turned out white Poms - they held four apiece. Each dog had its own individual attire, white, red, blue, or green silk bows around their hair and a lead and collar to match.

We stopped in our tracks. We didn't know whether to curtsey or bow. They looked the epitome of elegance. Surely they must be Royalty? Or at the very least landed gentry? Had they just arrived back from Cruft's? People from all over the neighbourhood rushed to their windows and lifted the curtains to make certain they didn't miss this parade of sheer indulgence and untold luxury.

But boy, oh boy, were we in for a shock as they drew even nearer. Even so they could have passed us by with hardly a disdainful look if at the moment of passing the gentleman hadn't raised his hat to us with the greeting 'Good morning, boys. A very nice morning too.'

He then took a black grubby finger out of an immaculate grey glove and, waving it under our noses continued, 'Now don't be late tonight, mustn't let the side down you know. Punctuality and hard work are of paramount importance. I wish you a very good morning.'

With that he replaced the starched grey glove and his hat, took his wife's arm and with an imperious swish of his coat-tails they swept on their way, leaving in their wake total disbelief and utter astonishment.

My mate, Walt Haynes, stood looking after their retreating figures, eyes popping out of his head, a look of pure incredulity mirrored in his face.

'Jack,' he whispered, 'it can't be! It wasn't! Tell me I'm mistaken! It wasn't who I thought it was - was it?'

I had to nod my head. 'It was. It was Old Bill and Big Bessy. Look, you can tell by his feet. Nobody I know walks like that but Old Bill.'

We looked after them as they sauntered up the path, his feet splayed out to a ninety-degree angle as he escorted Big Bessy. No one, but no one apart from Old Bill waddled along like a pregnant duck. Needless to say, Old Bill and Big Bessy were looked upon in a very different light from that day on. The old saying that you can't make a silk purse out of a sow's ear had been well and truly sunk without trace.

2
LEARNING MY TRADE

My first year was spent in learning all the different and complicated controls that were the responsibility of the firemen on a steam engine, as well as any other tasks that the foreman set us to do. We had by this time been issued with our LMS footplateman's uniform, which consisted of bib-and-brace overalls, a serge jacket, an overcoat and the distinctive shiny-topped peaked cap that was the hallmark of all train crews. We had also by this time gone over on to the three-shift system: days, afternoons and nights. It was the night shift that we enjoyed the most because after two or three hours work we would disappear on to any engine that was in steam and there, nice and warm, we would have our snap and yarn away the hours or nod off. The night foreman was not as young or as nimble as Mr Barnacle, thus giving us the chance to be off and away before he could reach us.

Also on the night shift we were often pressed into service as a 'knocker-up', for it was the custom in those days for all drivers, firemen and guards who were due to sign on between midnight and 6 am, and who lived within a three-mile radius of the Loco, to be knocked up one hour before they were due to sign on for duty. A large engine side-rod cotter-pin was used for this purpose. At that time I was very naive (a situation that was very soon to be rectified, for the railway was a veritable 'melting pot' regarding the seamier side of life, namely beer, baccy, and women, and not necessarily in that order). I could never understand why it always took such a great amount of banging on the doors to wake up the young firemen that had just got married. They no doubt had not even gone to sleep when I arrived with my cotter-pin to disturb them at whatever they were doing. I acquired a lot of new names that were shouted at me through bedroom windows!

It was towards the end of this first year that we took our first real step into the future. We were all tested individually by one of the dreaded 'bowler hat brigade', a Motive Power Inspector, on the knowledge that we had gained, the purpose being to gauge our suitability as future firemen. Whenever we saw someone wearing a bowler hat approaching we were always very apprehensive for it usually meant trouble of one kind or another.

I was taken on the footplate by the Inspector and asked to name the various controls and instruments, then to demonstrate the ones appertaining to the fireman. First there were the two live steam injectors that served to inject water into the boiler. These were, without doubt, the most important controls on the engine. If for some reason either one or both of these failed, you would be in serious trouble; the level of water remaining in the boiler would fall quite rapidly below the level of two lead-filled plugs located in the crown of the firebox and then, in theory, the lead would melt and allow the remaining water and steam to flood into the firebox and put out the fire. With anything up to half a ton of white hot fire you can imagine the indescribable mess that would follow.

Next there was the handbrake for use when the engine was stationary or to help slowing down when descending steep gradients. Other controls were the blower, which was used to draw the fire when the engine was coasting along without steam on; the dampers beneath the firebox, which admitted air through the fire; and the water scoop, which was used to pick up water from troughs spaced at intervals all along the main lines. You had to be very quick with this latter gear for you only had about 20 seconds in which to pick up between two and four thousand gallons before winding in the gear sharply before it was lost, quite possibly with disastrous consequences. Then there were two gauge glasses, which told you the level of water in the boiler, apart from many other gauges and levers too numerous to mention, but detailed in the accompanying diagram. The majority of the other main controls with which we had to be conversant in case of emergency were, of course, the responsibility of the driver, whether it was a left-hand or a right-hand drive (all the more recent, and therefore modern, engines were left-hand drive).

The main driver's controls were the regulator, which admitted steam into the cylinders, the reversing quadrant, which determined whether the engine went forward or backward, the vacuum-controlled steam brake, and the large and small ejectors, the function of which was to extract air from the continuous brake pipes and cylinders of whatever type of train you were coupled up to, whether it be a passenger express or a fully fitted freight train. This was a fail-safe system, for the whole of the braking system would be running under a partial vacuum, so whoever or whatever destroyed that vacuum would apply the brakes. This could happen either through the driver's or the guard's brake levers or the communication cord being pulled, or if the coupling broke, thus pulling the vacuum pipes apart.

The only other two items of importance were the whistle and the steam pressure gauge. The boilers of all the older engines were pressed at 175 pounds per square inch, but the larger and more modern ones were pressed at 225 pounds to a square inch, which made them very powerful indeed.

The examination was brought to its close by questions being put to us regarding the theoretical aspects of the relevant engine controls. All of these were included in the engineman's black book with which we had all been issued, together with the LMS Rule Book containing just over 200 rules with which we had to be conversant. For the moment, however, the only two that were really important were Rule 55 and Rule 179.

Rule 55 concerned the protection of your train when you were brought to a halt at a stop signal by the signalman. It was then the fireman's duty to sound the whistle and, if the signal was not immediately pulled off, to alight from the train and proceed to the signal box, inform the 'bobby' of your presence at his signal, sign the register and make sure he put a protective clamp on the lever of the signal behind your train. This prevented him from pulling it off and allowing another train to dash into the back of yours.

Rule 179, the most important in the Rule Book, was introduced to cover the unlikely possibility of your train becoming derailed when on any main line - it only happened to me twice in fifteen years as a fireman. You had to face the possibility that if you were unfortunate enough to come off the line you may run foul of the opposite line. You could then have traffic coming from the opposite direction running head on into your train, and if it happened to be an express or fitted freight at 60 or 70 miles per hour, the ensuing tragedy that would occur would be catastrophic.

In the event of derailment it was therefore the fireman's immediate duty to go forward on the opposite line with a red flag in daylight or a red lamp at night, together with a can of detonators, and stop any oncoming train. If a train was not imminent, you had to clip one detonator at a quarter of a mile, one at a half and three at three-quarters of a mile, not less than ten yards apart. But if by ill chance you happened to have a train piling in on you at that precise moment, all you would have time to do was run as near to it as you dare, slip three detonators down and get the hell out of it. Fast. In reality there were only two things the startled driver could do on hearing those three detonations. Slam his brake hard across - and pray.

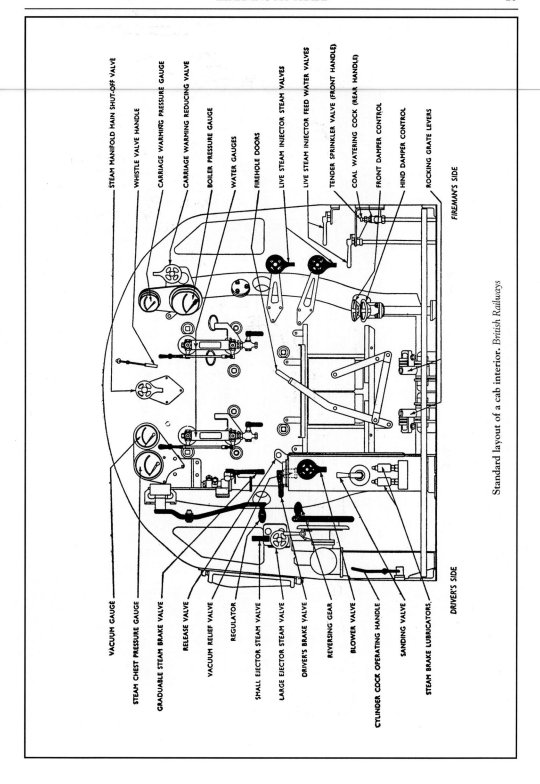

STEAM MANIFOLD MAIN SHUT-OFF VALVE

WHISTLE VALVE HANDLE

CARRIAGE WARMING PRESSURE GAUGE

CARRIAGE WARMING REDUCING VALVE

BOILER PRESSURE GAUGE

WATER GAUGES

FIREHOLE DOORS

LIVE STEAM INJECTOR STEAM VALVES

LIVE STEAM INJECTOR FEED WATER VALVES

TENDER SPRINKLER VALVE (FRONT HANDLE)

COAL WATERING COCK (REAR HANDLE)

FRONT DAMPER CONTROL

HIND DAMPER CONTROL

ROCKING GRATE LEVERS

FIREMAN'S SIDE

VACUUM GAUGE

STEAM CHEST PRESSURE GAUGE

GRADUABLE STEAM BRAKE VALVE

RELEASE VALVE

VACUUM RELIEF VALVE

REGULATOR

SMALL EJECTOR STEAM VALVE

LARGE EJECTOR STEAM VALVE

DRIVER'S BRAKE VALVE

REVERSING GEAR

BLOWER VALVE

CYLINDER COCK OPERATING HANDLE

SANDING VALVE

STEAM BRAKE LUBRICATORS

DRIVER'S SIDE

Standard layout of a cab interior. *British Railways*

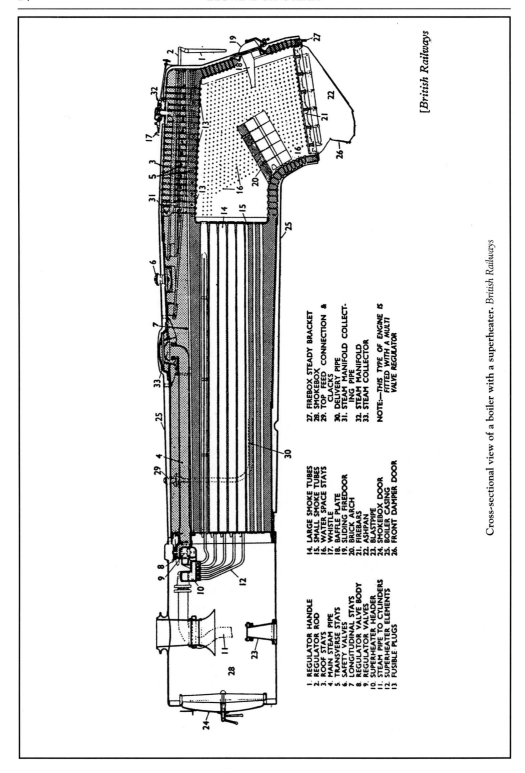

[*British Railways*]

1. REGULATOR HANDLE
2. REGULATOR ROD
3. ROOF STAYS
4. MAIN STEAM PIPE
5. TRANSVERSE STAYS
6. SAFETY VALVES
7. LONGITUDINAL STAYS
8. REGULATOR VALVE BODY
9. REGULATOR VALVES
10. SUPERHEATER HEADER
11. STEAM PIPE TO CYLINDERS
12. SUPERHEATER ELEMENTS
13. FUSIBLE PLUGS

14. LARGE SMOKE TUBES
15. SMALL SMOKE TUBES
16. WATER SPACE STAYS
17. WHISTLE
18. BAFFLE PLATE
19. SLIDING FIREDOOR
20. BRICK ARCH
21. FIREBARS
22. ASHPAN
23. BLASTPIPE
24. SMOKEBOX DOOR
25. BOILER CASING
26. FRONT DAMPER DOOR

27. FIREBOX STEADY BRACKET
28. SMOKEBOX
29. TOP FEED CONNECTION & CLACKS
30. DELIVERY PIPE
31. STEAM MANIFOLD COLLECT-ING PIPE
32. STEAM MANIFOLD
33. STEAM COLLECTOR

NOTE:—THIS TYPE OF ENGINE IS FITTED WITH A MULTI VALVE REGULATOR

Cross-sectional view of a boiler with a superheater. *British Railways*

3
THE NOVICE

I evidently must have satisfied the Inspector with all my answers on the theoretical side that day, as well as my application on the practical aspects. So, indeed, had all my fellow cleaners, for he informed us collectively that as from that moment we would have bestowed upon us the honorary title of 'Passed Cleaners'. No extra pay, of course, but what this did mean was that although in the immediate future we would generally be working much the same as before, as time went by and we gained more experience we would be eligible to take our place on the footplate as firemen when firing turns became available. Hooray! We had made it at last.

The method used to create an extra set of men was by splitting up an existing crew of driver and passed fireman. The latter would be a man who had passed an examination making him eligible to take his place as a driver whenever an extra crew was needed. A passed cleaner would be allocated to each of these drivers, thus completing the quartet. The requirement for an extra crew was more or less an everyday occurrence due to sickness and holidays, but, as is often the case, the unexpected was to happen and we were to be precipitated into the future more rapidly than we could have imagined.

By this time the war was two years old and although it was having very little noticeable effect on the efficiency of the railways as yet, things were to become rapidly worse as the war progressed.

It made its presence felt in two different ways. The first was that although strictly according to the rules no footplate staff were allowed to join the armed forces, one way or another several managed to do so. In fact, quite a lot of them were army reservists, but within the first two years the great majority had been called back on to the footplate. There were many grades of railwaymen that were called up into the forces, but they were mainly employed on the type of duties where they could be replaced by women, such as porters, office staff and, in a few cases, signalmen. The footplate, though, was no job for a woman, so for a certain amount of time we were short staffed.

The other reason was that as well as having a very busy programme of normal trains to run, the service was increasingly being intensified by the introduction of many extra emergency and priority services such as troop trains, hospital trains, ammunition trains and, as time went by, prisoner of war trains. What the majority of people lose sight of nowadays is that at this period the only means of transport substantially was by rail. There was no such things as motorways then, and the great roadway systems as we know them just did not exist. This was the reason why the Royal Air Force and the Luftwaffe tried so desperately to knock out the opposing railway systems, for if they could have succeeded in doing so the whole countries would have been paralysed.

One of the strict rules of the railway was that a driver or passed fireman could only drive over sections of the line that they had 'signed for'. This meant that they had either worked or travelled as a passenger over this section on an engine as many times as was necessary to know thoroughly not only all the signals on the main line but all those on the goods line as well, if it was a stretch with a four-track permanent way; sometimes it was possible that even an express would be turned on to a slow line if there had been an accident, if the track was being re-ballasted, or for a myriad of other reasons.

Some of the other firemen would often take a bit of a chance in that they would sign for a road over which they had not travelled often enough, thus making them eligible for a driving turn where other men would be passed by. The reason they used to take this gamble was that the more driving turns they did, the higher the rate of pay they were on. They used to rely on having the regular fireman on these trips who would know the road. The usual drill was that they would ask the fireman to take over the driving and were quite happy to do the firing. However, at times they would come unstuck if, for some reason, they did not have the regular fireman that was usually booked on the job.

The variety of firing duties to which all of the young-hand firemen were allotted consisted of, in the main, shed duties, disposing work, shunting, and local freight trains. There was always one set of men on the shed throughout the 24 hours, but it did not make much difference which shift you were on - the duties were fairly similar. Mainly they consisted of coaling and watering the engines. This could mean anything from four to ten tons of coal, depending on which route the locos were booked on, and around 3,500 gallons of water. We would then arrange the engines in the loco in the correct order of departure.

I always used to enjoy the shed duties because the foreman had no jurisdiction and you were in the sole care of the driver. Once we had got to know each other, I would take one engine and the driver another, and we would complete one each until we had them all sorted out. This meant a lot of hard work for four or five hours, but after that we were straight up, and the rest of the time was our own. It was a very nice feeling when the foreman came into the mess room, as was his habit about every half hour to clear out all the cleaners who were not supposed to be

there, and was obliged to leave you alone as you were on firing duties.

When you were booked on disposing work you would either relieve the set of men as they came on to the Loco, or somewhere just outside, then take their engine over the ashpit and clean the fire with the tools carried on all of them. Some of the fires would be in a terrible state if the engine had been on a long hard run. The clinker would be about a foot thick on the firebars and it all had to be broken up and lifted out. We also had to crawl underneath into the ashpit and rake out the damper box and then climb up and open the smokebox door and clean out all the ash that the blast from the exhausted steam from the cylinders had drawn through the tubes out of the firebox and through the boiler.

Incidentally, it was this blast that created the sharp deafening sound that reached such a crescendo of a continuous roar when you were working an engine very hard; it would draw the fire into a blinding white blur by causing a partial vacuum in the smokebox and cause air to be drawn via the dampers through the fire at a terrific pace to try and destroy that vacuum. Although you would be using a tremendous amount of steam as you thundered along, the white-hot fire would be generating fresh steam as quickly as you exhausted it. At least, this was the theory of the situation, but as we were to discover many times over in the future, the facts of the case could be very different.

When we were allocated to one of the shunting teams we would either take a small 'Jocko', as we used to call the shunters, off the Loco or make our way down to one of the shunting yards and relieve a set of men. Usually the drivers who were booked on this type of duty were either near retiring age or convalescing after an illness or accident. Our job would be to sort out the wagons, making them up into through trains going to far-flung places all over the country. The engines would then be coupled up and away they would steam - north, east, south, west. All very exciting to us at the time.

Sometimes we were fortunate enough to be allocated to one of the local freight trains.

A typical 'Jocko' shunting engine: 'Jinty' 0-6-0T No 47415, seen here on station pilot duties at Carlisle Citadel. *Mac Johnstone*

They never used to travel far from our own Loco, about ten or twenty miles in any direction, and our task was to take empty wagons or vans into the various sidings belonging to the bigger manufacturing companies, and exchange them for loaded ones for despatch to the nearest shunting sidings. We looked forward to these trips because they always took us on to new ground and we would see some of the countryside that not many people were fortunate enough to see.

The reason for this was that the great majority of the railway ran through very lonely and quiet terrain and it was only when you ran into towns and cities that you would begin to see signs of life. One of our local freight workings took us down the single-line branch to Southwell. This was one of our favourite runs, giving us plenty of time to leave the engine when we were shunting in the local sidings; depending on the time of the year, we knew all the best spots to find wild flowers such as bluebells and cowslips, and also where all the best mushrooms, bluestalks and blackberries could be picked. Many was the time I would go home loaded down with one or the other, or an armful of wild flowers. These occasions were very often

extra to normal service, so we would usually be booked with a young-hand passed fireman, only about ten years or so older than ourselves, and we would both have a sense of freedom which added to the novelty of the situation.

We would enjoy a nice, leisurely snap time with the guard to keep us company. It was surprising the topics of conversation in which we would get involved - politics, sport, Rules and Regulations - not forgetting the big three, beer, baccy, and women! Little did we know at the time that we were in the heyday of our careers. The days of hard work and long travel had not descended upon us yet, for we were young and still in the process of learning to master our art. Believe me, that's what being an efficient train crew really was, and that is no overstatement!

By this time I had learned to read the signals. They were very complex and all different, depending on which section you were passing through, but they all gave the same message once you had sorted out the ones

To stop an express train running at 60 or 70 mph, such as this one behind LMS 'Pacific' No 6208 at Brinklow on the West Coast Main Line in April 1939, would take two to three miles. . .

. . .and a loose coupled freight train without a continuous brake required great skill from the footplate crew and guard to keep it under control on a gradient. Here an ex-LNWR 0-8-0 hauls its long mineral train up on to the Northampton loop at Hilmorton, near Rugby, in August 1938. *Both G. A. Barlow, Mac Johnstone collection*

that belonged to you from the ones that did not. For instance, if you were routed main line, you ignored the goods line signals, and vice versa. It was a case of concentrating on your own particular signals and ignoring the rest.

This was no mean feat when you consider that some of the gantries could have upwards of twenty signals or more, and if you were travelling at 60 or 70 miles per hour you would only have a few seconds in which to spot yours - not too difficult in daylight, but at night it was like looking at a Christmas tree. The number of signals for each section would depend on the size of the junction or station. They always started with a distant signal, which was coloured yellow and black, and this could be some distance from the signal box. This was not a stop signal and could be passed at danger, but it repeated the signals in advance of it, which *were* the stop signals and were red and white for easy identification. The procedure was that if you had the distant 'off', this would mean all the stop signals in advance of you for that section were also off, so you could proceed in confidence, even in thick fog.

Express and ordinary passenger trains had at least two or three sections clear ahead, and you very often needed every yard, depending on the gradient. To stop an express train, which in total could weigh upwards of 500 tons, travelling at 70 miles an hour, you would need at least two to three miles before you started to get it under control.

It was just as important, but for a different reason, for a goods or coal train to have this advance warning, for whereas neither of these types of train would achieve the speed of an express, this was more than compensat-ed for by the fact that when you applied the brake on a passenger train it was a continuous brake throughout - with a coal train you were utterly dependent on the engine brake, with some assistance from the one in the guard's van which was pretty useless anyway to help stop 50 or 60 wagons.

If you were running along a level gradient you could judge and control your train far more readily than if you were on a downhill stretch, when the position, to say the least, could be very hazardous. Whatever the type of engine you had been given, be it a Class '3', '4' or one of the powerful new '8' freights, the guard would be duty bound to load you to the limit the engine could safely manage on the steepest stretch of the line along which you were due to travel. When the powers that be worked out the maximum for any particular type of engine, the tests were always carried out on a fine day using a new engine from the repair shops at Derby, with everything in first class condition. It was very rare, in practice, for these combinations to come together, hence the thrills, spills and runaways that were the common everyday lot of the footplate staff.

Many times these hazards were to become reality in the future, for our Loco was situated amongst a conglomeration of steep banks and tunnels. On many of our heavy coal trains we used to have a 'pilot', the name given to an engine hooked up in front of a train engine, thus making you into a double-header, or conversely an engine that hooked up to the back of the train to push you over the steepest sections; this was known as a banker. Apart from such occasional help you were on your own, and the best of luck, which you very often needed.

4
BAPTISM OF FIRE

It was due to another of the railway's inflexible rules that I was to have a very sharp foretaste of what a real fireman's day consisted of - not just playing at it, which is really all we had been doing so far. The rule in question was that everyone had to abide by the fact that if your employment with the LMS commenced just one day before any of your fellow firemen, you were considered an older hand. Conversely, if you started one day later, you were the younger hand. Everything was taken in strict seniority and there was no deviation from this rule under any circumstances.

I had been employed on the railway for about a year by this time and had been out on 40 or 50 firing turns, all on local duties, when one morning at eleven o'clock, having signed on at eight o'clock for a day's cleaning, the foreman called me into his office and ordered me collect all my kit and hurry down to Mansfield Station where I would find Tom Roper waiting for me. His regular fireman had been taken ill, and I was the oldest hand available so had to take his place. Initially I couldn't take in this earth-shattering news. Normally no fireman was allowed on a passenger job until he had at least a couple of years of firing experience, and I had a pretty good idea that this particular job was the hardest of both of the passenger links at my home depot.

With hindsight I now realise that this was the best thing that could have happened to me, to be thrown in at the deep end, for I didn't have time to worry about it, just get on with it. I arrived at the station in double quick time and climbed up on to the footplate of No 424, an ex-Midland Class '2' passenger engine. It was blessed with 8-foot driving wheels and was noted for not being a particularly strong engine, but it was most certainly a very fast one.

Tom Roper scrutinised me as though I'd just crawled out of the floorboards and rasped 'Who are you?'

'I'm your fireman, Mr Roper,' I replied hesitantly, shaking like a leaf.

'In the first place,' he growled, 'my name is not Mr Roper, it's Tom. In the second place, are you any good?'

Not a very good start to the day, I mused silently.

'Well, I think I can manage Mr Roper - Tom - I'll try my hardest.'

'Well, we'll see what you shape up like, and if you don't do the job to my satisfaction I'll phone through to Nottingham for another fireman.'

Now, although the firing I had done over the past year and this present day's work were basically similar, where they differed was in that on a coal train if you did happen to drop a clanger you would usually have time to put things right. On a passenger train everything had to be done so much more quickly, and there was no time to rectify mistakes. In other words, you had to get it right first time!

These Class '2s' were only pressed at 160 pounds per square inch and I was conscious of the fact that if I allowed the steam pressure to fall below 120 pounds per square inch there wouldn't be enough power left for the ejector to hold the brakes off on the coaches and they would inevitably pull you to a halt. If this mishap did befall you, especially

A British Railways view of a Midland Class '2' 4-4-0, formerly No 553, one of the 'long legged ones' of the same class that gave me my 'baptism of fire' with Tom Roper. Wellingborough, February 1956. *Derek Murdoch*

between sections or stations, you were in serious trouble indeed, for it would entail making out reports, a real earwigging from the foreman or, at worst, a trip to Derby to confront 'God', as the General Manager was known to the hoi polloi. All these problems had been flitting through my mind as I'd been rushing down to the station - and we hadn't even started yet.

I only had ten minutes left before we got the 'right away' from the guard, so my first task was to put a good fire on and make sure the boiler was full, for a good start was essential. But you had to time things right, for you were not allowed to make smoke in the station nor allow the steam pressure to go beyond the red danger mark on the steam gauge, which would cause the relief valves to pop open, known to all footplate staff as 'blowing off'. I built the fire up across the back of the firebox whilst keeping it thin along the front, for it was placing coal there that produced smoke; you therefore always left this manoeuvre until the last few seconds.

Eleven twenty-six, one minute to go. Nine or ten shovels placed strategically down the sides and at the front, box her up, then switch on the blower to draw the fire to a white hot glow. The needle quivers on the red mark and we get the green flag and a piercing whistle from the guard.

We're off, dead on 11.27 to start the first leg of our journey stopping at all stations to Ambergate, 25 miles distant. Our first stop was Sutton Junction, five miles away and all uphill. The line was wet and greasy, causing us to slip as we struggled to get away, so Tom switched on the steam sanders to gain traction. After a couple of miles we were fairly belting along and the noise on the footplate caused by the blast of steam being exhausted through the chimney and the ringing of the engine wheels on the line was indescribable.

Surely this can't be normal, I mused, but Tom seemed to be quite happy with the flaming row. We were also lurching all over the place due to the thrust of the pistons in the cylinders, first one side then the other.

To make matters even worse, the engine and tender were not a single unit but merely coupled together via a steel leaf-plate across the joint. This tended to promote a see-saw effect giving you the impression you were having a free ride on the dodgems at the local fair. The fireman had no option but to stand on this leaf-plate and try to keep his balance whilst stoking the fire; this was no easy task.

What you also had to take into account was that when the engine was working heavily it was bad practice to open the firebox doors to their full extent. This would allow an undue amount of cold air to be drawn into the firebox, causing the steam pressure to drop. The only way round this problem was to keep the air deflector in place just inside the doors, then only open them half way. This gave you a space of six to nine inches to fire through, and a very tricky operation it was too when you consider that you didn't just throw the coal in but had to place it in the back corners, down the sides and across the front - never in the middle, or the engine wouldn't steam properly. You had to know exactly where in the firebox the fire needed building up, have all the coal cracked up into lumps no bigger than your fist, then have a few seconds only to open the doors, place the coal where the fire was thinnest at the rate of seven or eight shovels at a time, then box her up quickly.

Most of this knowledge was, as yet, just theory to me, and according to the experienced firemen it could take at least two years continual firing before it all dropped into place. I could well believe this, for it looked seemingly impossible at the time. If this trip did nothing else, it would show me just how much I still had to learn.

As we ran into Sutton I opened the firebox doors and switched on the blower. This had the effect of dissipating the smoke and knocking the pressure back slightly to prevent her blowing off. The platform was reasonably full of passengers with a couple of porters to supervise. We were allowed one or two minutes in the stations, depending on the work that needed to be done. There was always a great deal of parcel traffic on these trains, but once this had been exchanged and the passengers were all aboard, we got the green flag.

Next stop was Kirkby, and still uphill. I was beginning to get the hang of things by now, and it was the same drill as we thundered into the station. There was a level crossing here and we stopped with the engine right across it and crowds of people gathered about, all wanting to look at the engine. No wonder they used to call these the glamour jobs!

The next stretch was on a steep winding downhill line to Pinxton, then across the London-Scotland line at Pye Bridge. The last ten miles through Butterley to Ambergate was along the beautiful Amber Valley in Derbyshire. This was by far the prettiest stretch of track I was ever to work along, and, surely, Ambergate Station must be the most picturesque in the Midlands. It had a triangular platform set very high above the road, and the view from all three platforms was magnificent. All around the station were the lovely Derbyshire hills and forests that seemed to reach to the very sky. They were to be seen at their best in the spring with all the wild flowers and the foliage on the trees bursting into life; and again in the autumn, when the vista was a great splash of green and gold.

Ambergate was also a very important junction for, having three island platforms, trains would be converging upon it from three different directions: from the east, Sheffield and Leeds; from the west, Derby and Bristol; and from the north, Manchester. It was also very convenient for trains such as our own, for the triangular arrangement allowed us to run round it to be facing the direction from which we had just arrived and still be engine-first for the next part of our journey back to Pye Bridge, then through Chesterfield to Sheffield.

We had twenty minutes to complete this manoeuvre before we were again due away. The station was by now crowded as a result of the connections that had run in, so once more I had a good fire arranged in readiness.

By this time Tom had started to utter the occasional word to me in his gruff voice. I only hoped to God that from this I could

Kirkby Station, *circa* 1930.
Nottingham Evening Post

In 1950 a waiting room and a platform were destroyed by fire at
Ambergate Station. The photograph shows firemen clearing up
the debris. *Nottingham Evening Post*

assume that he would not be calling for a
fresh fireman from Nottingham. And then,
wonder of wonders, he even managed a half-
smile in my direction, which perked me up
no end.

Ten minutes to go. Just time for me to
snatch a sandwich, a mug of tea and a crafty
smoke. The time-honoured method of mashing a billy-can of tea was simplicity itself.
After carefully balancing the can on the lip
of the firebox, the intense heat from the fire
would have it boiling away within twenty
seconds. You needed two cans to complete
this 'Egon Ronay' trick properly. Having
popped the tea into the boiling water, you
would then leave it for five minutes to mash,

A view of the aqueduct that carried the Cromford Canal over the main LMS main line at Bull Bridge, Ambergate, an early engineering feat said to have solved a problem which confronted Stephenson when making the railway line.

A Midland Class '2' 4-4-0 is passing beneath. *Nottingham Evening Post*

then decant the brew into the second can, leaving the tea-leaves behind. The tea would then keep hot for hours on end without stewing.

Twelve forty-five. Doors slamming, porters bustling about, a green flag and a whistle from our guard and we were away, stopping at all stations to Sheffield.

Six shovels of black gold across the front, box her up, shut off the injector, and within the space of a few minutes we were bowling along at quite a brisk pace, retracing the same route to Pye Bridge, then up the steep Erewash Valley to the steel city of Sheffield.

After leaving Pye Bridge behind, the ground was all completely new to me, but Tom was helping me quite considerably by telling me the type of gradients that lay immediately ahead of us.

We next passed through Alfreton Tunnel. Now, I had passed through many tunnels before, but only on coal trains where, of course, you were proceeding at a more leisurely pace, and where the contrast between light and dark was nowhere near as drastic and immediate as being on a passenger engine belting along at 70 miles per hour. Moving out of bright sunlight into total darkness within the space of a split second produced a very eerie sensation. This was highlighted by the tremendous noise that was being bounced back at us off the walls and roof of the tunnel. At the best of times an engine running at speed would make one hell

of a row, but in the enclosed space of the tunnel it was increased tenfold.

We pulled into Chesterfield at 1.30, dead on time. We were allowed a full ten minutes before being due away, during which time the station staff sorted out passengers, luggage and parcels. I was very grateful for this short break as it enabled me to build up the fire, fill the boiler, and have a sweep round the footplate.

In general I was keeping on top of the job, but I had been making small mistakes - not important in themselves, but collectively they could have added up if allowed to. Details like making black smoke, blowing off steam, boiler pressure dropping, water level in the boiler not as high as I would have liked, and all these incidents were happening at the wrong time. It was lack of co-ordination on my part due to lack of experience - but I was learning fast.

By 1.40 we were pulling out on the last leg of this section of the day's work. It was hard pounding, but only three more stations to go then up through Dore & Totley tunnel before dropping down the bank into Sheffield, again bang on time! I know it must be difficult to imagine in these present days of frustration and delays, but in my day 95 per cent of passenger trains were always on time. It was considered by all conscientious drivers and firemen that one minute early was as bad as being one minute late!

Having shunted our train into a siding, we

now, unbelievably, had one whole hour before we were next due away on the return run from Sheffield to Nottingham. But during that hour we had many tasks to perform.

Firstly, we ran on to the turntable to spin the engine around. I then set about cleaning the fire of all the ash and clinker that had collected on the bars, topped up with about three thousand gallons of water, pulled all the coal that was piled high on the back of the tender down to the front, cracked it up ready for instant use, then the time remaining, about fifteen minutes, was my own. Just long enough for another bite and a mug of tea, now getting past its best but still tasting like nectar to me.

Sheffield was quite a large and busy station with crowds of people congregating on the platforms; the last-minute goodbyes, passengers boarding the coaches laden down with luggage on their way to catch other connections, possibly to far distant towns and cities, or making their way home after a hard day's work. Porters busying themselves loading parcels into the guard's van, and the familiar distinctive sound of the wheel-tapper's hammer as he went alongside the coaches - all these things I remember, the hustle and bustle, the norm on any main-line station just before a train was due out.

Meanwhile I had been preparing the engine for the hard slog out of Sheffield that preceded the long downhill stretch along the Erewash Valley and into Nottingham. We only had four miles of the steep bank to climb before reaching level gradients, and to the best of my ability No 424 was as ready as she would ever be. I had 2 feet of white-hot fire roaring away, a boiler full of water, and the steam pressure relief valves were beginning to hiss and pop as we got the 'right away' at 3.45.

We were soon blasting away up the bank having got a good start on the, by now, dry line, and I was now getting used to the noise and motion of the engine, nowhere near as apprehensive as when I had first set foot on her. And yes, I was actually beginning to

Dealing the coal in the tender whenever you had a spare moment was an important job. Here the fireman of ex-Midland 0-6-0 No 3551 climbs on to the coal, perhaps to crack up a few of the larger pieces. Note also the single headlamp on the bracket in front of the chimney, denoting an ordinary passenger train. Nottingham Midland, July 1937. G. A. Barlow, Mac Johnstone collection

enjoy myself, with the added attraction of a job well done. But I was still keeping my fingers crossed - I still hadn't forgotten the words Tom had growled at me when I first stepped aboard the footplate in Mansfield regarding his threat to send for a fresh fireman if I didn't measure up.

We had clear signals all the way down the Erewash Valley; this was normal procedure, for the signalman always kept the main line free for passenger trains by switching slower traffic on to the goods lines. We were thus able to keep good time, which was as well for we had a very tight schedule; due into Nottingham at 5.15, and out again at 5.30, we couldn't afford any signal checks.

Dusk had begun to fall by the time we were half way into our journey, but I had already lit the two headlamps, one of which I had placed on the chimney bracket up front which was the code denoting a passenger train to all concerned. The second lamp I retained on the footplate as a spare. The only other lamp to be lit was the one that hung on a bracket at the side of the gauge glass to illuminate the level of water in the boiler.

At 5.15 on the dot, having stopped at approximately twenty stations since leaving Sheffield and exchanging passengers, goods and parcels *en route*, we ran through Wilford Road Junction into number 2 platform in Nottingham.

We were promptly relieved by a new set of men. We gathered our belongings together and hurried across to number 5 platform where we in turn relieved another Nottingham crew on a Midland Class '3' tank engine with which we were due to work up the heavy bank to Mansfield on the last leg of our journey. These Stanier 'tankies' were nowhere near as fast as the larger class we had just given up, having smaller driving wheels, but they were much more powerful. Just the type for hauling a heavy passenger train over a steep bank.

Only ten more stations to go and we would have completed our day's work. Level running for the first five miles, then up the hill, through Annesley Tunnel and drop down into Mansfield from where our journey had originated seven and a half hours previously. It seemed like seven and a half days to me! I had never been so pleased to see my home station in my life - I was absolutely whacked. We shunted the carriages into the sidings, unhooked the engine and took it on to the Loco where we signed off to complete our eight-hour shift.

Tom had uttered very few words to me during our day together on the footplate, but in the presence of our Loco foreman, Sam Maltby, I overheard snatches of their conversation regarding myself. One of the remarks I caught gave me great comfort for the future.

'Bearing in mind the amount of experience he's had, he did very well indeed. . .'

This was praise unlimited from an old timer like Tom!

During our eight-hour shift we had burned about six tons of coal, used approximately six thousand gallons of water, travelled around 120 miles, and stopped at 48 stations. In short, it had been eight hours of slog and sweat.

But this was just one day's toil in a fireman's six-day week. And for this he was paid the princely sum of three pounds ten shillings a week. And that was for a fireman on the top rate of pay.

5
BATTLE OF THE TITANS

During 1942 the war began to take its toll. There was minimum maintenance on engines and rolling-stock and due to the shortage of footplate staff any Loco that had a manpower surplus - and for a period of about eight months we at Mansfield came into that category - used to send firemen that were extra to requirements to other Midland Locos that were short-staffed to man the many extra trains that were needed to maintain the war effort. This stretched the railway's manpower situation to its very limit. Many firemen were sent to other Locos as the need arose for either one or two days, or even for weeks at a time. These extra duties were very flexible, depending on the urgency of the traffic involved.

I personally had several days at Wellingborough and Cricklewood, where we lodged in the not too salubrious railway hostels; but in those difficult days a clean bed and a hot meal was indeed welcome after a hard day's work firing for anything up to twelve or fourteen hours at a time. If the Loco was near at hand, for example Nottingham or Kirkby, you would travel passenger there, do your day's work, then make your own way home. This made for a long day, but anything was preferable to those infamous railway lodges.

Several of the firing turns I was booked on from Kirkby Loco proved most interesting, the reason being that my own depot at Mansfield was a mixed freight and passenger depot where, due to the strict time-keeping mentality that all our train crews had grown up with, we always made a conscious effort to keep to time no matter

which type of train we were working on. The attitude of the crews at Kirkby was entirely different.

Although there were timetables laid down for the running of coal trains, they were rarely kept to. Many of the reasons, of course, were out of the engineman's hands, such as bad weather, lack of maintenance due to manpower shortage, passenger trains being given priority over goods engines, second grade coal which caused steaming problems, and a myriad of other causes which befell all large depots. The general attitude of the crews at Kirkby was that provided the work was carried through, the time it took was immaterial, whether it took hours or even days. Whereas we at Mansfield would turn up for work with enough provisions to last us a normal shift, give or take a few hours, the Kirkby men would arrive with enough groceries to tide them over for several days. They would have packed into their enginemen's boxes a couple of loaves, half pounds each of butter and cheese, and a quarter pound of tea with the corresponding amounts of sugar and milk to provide them with endless brews.

I was very soon to see the wisdom of their thinking, for 90 per cent of Kirkby's workload was hauling coal trains out of the East Midlands collieries to far-flung destinations, then working the empty wagons back home again on the return journey. For these extremely heavy trains they manned, in the main, powerful LMS Class '8' freight engines. They had eight coupled wheels that provided plenty of traction and adequate braking power and they generally steamed well if you

A post-war, BR period view of Kirkby loco shed (16C). On shed, left to right, are ex-LMS Class '8F' 2-8-0 No 48270, ex-WD Class '8F' 2-8-0 No 90682, and another ex-LMS '8F', No 48193. August 1955. *Derek Murdoch*

could keep a box full of fire, but very often, when working heavy, they'd blast the fire through the chimney end as fast as you could stoke it.

I fired on several trips to Wellingborough, and invariably on these trips we would keep somewhere near to time, for with this being

LMS '8F' No 8492 working hard on the up goods line just north of Wellingborough Station in September 1947. The building in the left background is the enginemen's lodging house. *K. C. H. Fairey*

the main line to London from the Midlands there was an up and down main plus an extra set of goods lines. It was the goods lines that we usually ran on, but sometimes, between expresses, they would push us out main line for short stretches which meant you really had to hop along to the next junction otherwise you were in danger of slowing down an express that was on your tail. At Wellingborough we would be relieved by another set of men who would take the train forward to London.

One of the trips in particular remains stark in my mind. Not that there was anything to suggest the unusual was about to unfold in the innocently worded signing-on slip delivered to my home by one of the junior 'knockers-up'. I was to sign on at 6.45 pm, catch the 7.20 passenger train to Kirkby and present myself to the foreman for duty at Kirkby Loco. Furthermore I was to be prepared to lodge for the night and work back the following day.

'That's fine,' I shrugged. 'Be a pleasant change from the run-of-the-mill jobs in and around Mansfield.'

It certainly turned out to be a change alright.

Whether it was a pleasant change was, and still is, debatable. No more information was forthcoming when I looked in at my home depot, so I took myself off down to the station. On reaching Kirkby my first inclination was to seek out my dad, 'Darky'. I soon found him in the fitting shop with his mates and informed him why I was trespassing on his happy hunting ground.

'Better take yourself off then, lad, and see what job you're on.'

I was back within five minutes.

'I'm booked on your 8.20 Wellingborough and lodge.'

My father looked at me sideways and raised his voice slightly over the hubbub and conversation of the assembled fitters.

'Who's your driver?'

'Jock Bowen's his name, Dad, but I must admit I don't know him.'

The name Jock Bowen stopped all conversation. A dozen pairs of eyes turned slowly towards me. An apprehensive look spread across my father's face.

'Jock Bowen, eh?'

'Yes, Dad. Anything wrong?'

'No, lad. No. You'll be alright.' But there was an inflexion in his voice that belied his words. The fragmented conversations started up again, more muted with sidelong glances at me and my father.

'Come with me, lad,' he said, 'I'll help you find him.'

But once outside he stopped me in my tracks. His voice was low, even and serious.

'Now, with Jock,' he warned, 'you do as you are told. You behave yourself. Understand?'

I started to worry, to feel uneasy. I nodded my agreement because in those days, even at twenty, you obeyed your father or faced the consequences. My father was a hard man but a fair man, and I always respected and took his advice.

'Good. He'll be in the messroom - I'll introduce you to him.'

Once inside the messroom my father motioned for me to follow him and strode across to the far end. He stopped at the last table and looked down at a seated man of around fifty years of age.

'Jock, this is my son. I believe he's your fireman for the next two days.'

Jock Bowen looked at me with sharp penetrating eyes that missed nothing. The uneasiness in my stomach began to grow as I got the distinct feeling that no one ever crossed this man and got away with it. Although his voice was guarded in the presence of my father, I received a premonition that this was to be no ordinary trip.

'Hope you can cope, lad,' he rasped, 'I don't hang about!'

My father searched my eyes knowing that any answer to Jock Bowen must come from me. But I was growing up fast in this hard school and learning every day.

'I can cope, Jock,' I said evenly. 'I've done this run several times before.'

He looked me up and down and appreciated an honest answer. When he stood, his voice softened slightly.

'Good lad. I'll look after him, Darky,' he reassured my father. Turning back to me he said, 'Come on Jack, let's see what engine we've got.'

It was on the destination board. Eight-fifteen Wellingborough. It was to be No 8096, one of the aforementioned LMS Class '8' freight, a comparatively new breed of Staniers. Two cylinders, 2-8-0 wheel arrangement, 4 ft 8½ in driving wheels, pressed at 225 pounds per square inch. With this amount of super-heated steam punching into the cylinders, believe me it could pull a house down.

She was engine prepared so all we needed

LMS Stanier Class '8F' 2-8-0 No 8076, numerically
close to that on which I fired for Jock Bowen. The
engine is seen here on the West Coast Main Line at
Hillmorton, near Rugby, on 15 August 1938. G. A.
Barlow, Mac Johnstone collection

to do was give her a quick check over then
make our way to Kirkby Up Sidings to hook
up to our block train of loaded coal wagons. I
stood back from the notice board for a few
seconds whilst Jock engaged in conversation
with one of his fellow drivers, and this gave
me the opportunity to study him in depth.

Small in stature, no more than five three,
the fierce waxed moustache made him look
hard, wiry, lean. Smart, dapper almost, with
the Midland's emblem on a polished peak
cap and an immaculate bib-and-brace uniform, black jacket, white shirt and black tie,
with shoes you could see your face in. He carried an engineman's steel box which would
contain relevant documents and, knowing
Kirkby men as I did, enough food to last for a
week if necessary.

But what the hell was he carrying under
his arm?

At first glance it looked like a huge block
of wood about eighteen inches in diameter
and six inches thick. All was to be revealed
shortly.

'Come on, Jack,' he called. 'Time we were
off. Must keep to time.'

Even with his short stature I was hard
pressed to keep pace with him as he strode
through the Loco and up the yard as though he
were a Sergeant Major at a passing-out parade.

Evidently new out of the Derby workshops
after her refit, 8096 stood resplendent at the
mouth of the turntable. We climbed aboard
and after checking that we had the obligatory
box of spanners, detonators and red flags, we
were ready for the off. Just time for a quick
glance at the water gauge, which told us that
we had a full tank, 4,500 gallons, then at the
tender to be sure it had been coaled properly.
It had. Full to its limit with eight tons of
bright, hard steam coal.

I suddenly heard a dull thud and turned to
see Jock standing on the block of wood as he
gave a piercing blast on the hooter. So that
was the reason for the mysterious chunk of
wood he'd kept tucked under his arm! He's so
short and stocky, and the whistle lever's so
high, he can't reach the damn thing!

But if he was a bit short in height, my God
he wasn't short in any other capacity, as I
was about to find out - to my cost.

The signal came off and with a whoosh of
steam from the still open cylinder taps we

were away like a greyhound out of its trap. Past the signal box, down to the sidings and hooked up to our train before you could say Jack Robinson - or even Jack Backen!

'How many on today, Sam?' Jock asked our guard, Sam Jones.

'Fifty-six,' he shouted. 'Full load!'

'My God, they've hung them on,' Jock rasped. 'What the hell do they think they're playing at? Think we can't handle 'em? Eh?'

Certainly they'd 'hung them on', but Jock Bowen didn't know why. Nor did I at the time, but was gleefully informed some time later.

The facts, briefly, were as follows. Whenever Control, known as 'God's minions' to us, discovered that Jock Bowen was the driver in charge, they always insisted, without question, that he be loaded up to the absolute maximum limit. No other driver but Jock ever received this personal attention. Why? It had long been Jock's proud boast, repeated many times over throughout the Midland Division of the LMS, that he had never, repeat, *never*, been bested in his profession as a top-link driver.

Not by any engine. Or any train, however heavily laden. Nor especially by that set of morons that sat on their big fat behinds in their plush offices, smoking their big fat cigars. The morons known as Control. So, through Jock's boasting, a one-sided battle of wits developed, with the awesome power of Control, who had the whole of the LMS running like scared rabbits, on the one hand, and the diminutive five-foot-three figure of the unsuspecting Jock Bowen on the other.

There was an air of expectancy in Nottingham Control, the general attitude of vicious optimism being 'We'll have him by the short and curlies this time. This will wipe the smirk off his face. Tonight we get him. Tonight Bowen tastes the bitter pill of defeat at the hand of Control.'

Wires were buzzing, telephones jangling. Nottingham Loco was instructed to keep a set of men handy to provide an immediate 'banker' if called upon.

Every signalman was ordered to report our progress on passing. The sombre figures in Control had assumed a new mantle. It was like Christmas all over again for them. They were smiling, slapping one another on the back. Joviality was the order of the day.

This was 'High Noon' in the Midlands, the gunfight at the OK Corral, the battle of Waterloo and the night we got Bowen all rolled into one!

The big decider, and the real test, would come over the ten-mile-long 1 in 200 bank that snaked its way out of Nottingham Station and through the suburbs of West Bridgford, Edwalton and Plumtree; then onwards through the long dark forbidding tunnels of Stanton and Grimston before the line levelled out then dropped down into the lovely old market town of Melton Mowbray.

But all this drama, all the 'get Jock Bowen' plotting and subterfuge still lay ahead of us as Jock, with a fierce blast on the hooter, shouted 'Are you ready Jack? Keep a good fire on, we're going to need it soon.'

This I well knew, so, like the proverbial boy scout, I was prepared.

There was no great urgency for at least an hour, as we had a long straight pull out of the sidings, followed by a two-mile slightly upward incline to the mouth of Annesley tunnel that led directly on to the steep downhill fifteen-mile stretch into Nottingham. Even so, I had a sharp foretaste of what lay in store, for instead of the gentle introduction of steam into the cylinders to tighten the couplings, Jock snapped the regulator halfway across instantly and 8096 leapt forward like a great black stallion of the night. The two-inch-thick solid steel couplings could be heard screeching their protest as they pulled tight, reverberating the whole length of the train.

The poor old guard, I grinned to myself. I hope he's got his seat belt on.

We thundered out of the sidings, through the crossing gates and were at the lip of the tunnel within minutes. Jock closed the regulator to allow the momentum to ease off, as the wagons would want some holding down the bank. But we were OK, 8096 was in good condition after her recent sojourn in the works at Derby, and at least, for a little while now, I could sit down, take stock and think matters through.

Even with my limited railway knowledge I

could sense that something was in the air! For instance, no one, but no one, ever loaded these trains down to the limit. They would always knock off nine or ten wagons in the interest of pure common sense. And why the hell the majority of Jock's firemen suddenly developed a case of flu or belly ache or Monday morning leg as soon as they learned they were on this particular job I couldn't for the life of me understand. It was strange, too, I realised, that the number of Grandmas that died under suspicious circumstances far exceeded the number of Grandmas that existed in the first place. Perhaps the firemen were borrowing any spare ones that were going cheap from Mansfield or Sutton to fill the gap. . .

Much later I was to learn the answers.

But that night something was in the air. I knew it, everyone else knew it, but, probably, not Jock Bowen, stood on his chunk of wood on the footplate of 8096.

All the regular firemen had it sussed out. This might well be the long-awaited trial of strength, of wills, between the powers that be and the diminutive, boastful Jock Bowen - a 1940s struggle between David and Goliath, a scaled-down battle of Verdun or the Somme, the Armageddon of the Midlands.

But the one person they all forgot in this great battle of minds and reputations was the poor bloody fireman! Jock didn't need one fireman, he needed two, three, maybe four, or a whole bloody battalion of them, all with shovels in both hands!

We rolled into the outer suburbs of Nottingham to a darkening sky. The Loco lay over to our right and the vast conglomerate of the shunting yards lay over to our left. The beautifully preserved outlines of Nottingham Castle stood out in relief against the skyline, its windows reflecting the deep red rays of the setting sun. Slowly we snaked our way through the confusing array of signals, up and down main, up and down goods, until we found our path.

There was a hush of expectancy in the air.

We glided almost silently over the crossing points, hardly a whisper emanating from 8096. She was trembling, anxious almost, as though fearful of what was about to unfold.

The little 'Jockos' in the shunting yard ceased their eternal puffing and quietly watched as we slipped by. There was no envy in their eyes for their giant sister. They urged her on - she was carrying the flag.

Could she do it? They held their breath and wished her well.

8096 seemed to grow in stature, to gird her loins. She knew. The little 'Jockos' knew. The watching signalmen with their telephones at the ready knew.

And Control knew.

The moment of truth was about to dawn. Any moment now and the silence of the night was about to be shattered. I was as ready as I ever could be. I had a pot full of water, a magnificent white-hot fire, and coal at the ready. I could do no more.

In all fairness they gave us the road. The tracks were clear. Off came the red and white stop signals, off flew the yellow fishtail distants.

Jock gave her half regulator through the deserted platforms of the station, under the road bridge and past the imposing London Road signal box where we hit the curve that led direct to the main London line. We accelerated quickly along the short downhill stretch before we hit the bank proper. Faster, ever faster to the rhythm of the engine and the wheels, then Jock gave her the lot, opened her right out.

Regulator right across. Valve gear fully open. My God, what thunder as 8096 dug her heels in! It seemed nothing could stop us now as the night sky was lit up by the flying cascade of white-hot sparks as they blasted from the chimney. I was already firing, firebox doors half open, air deflector in position. Ten quick flashes speared around the box, slam the doors shut to keep up the pressure, on with the injector to top up the boiler.

Out of the corner of my eye I could see Jock performing. He was in his element, bristling with pride with a satanic smile playing around his lips. He was hopping around like a kangaroo, checking this, checking that, a touch here, a touch there. He notched her up a couple of points as a reserve - we might need it. He jumped up on his wooden block, gave a blast on the whistle then hopped back to terra firma. He grinned in my direction as he mouthed the words over the deafening thunder of the engine: 'OK, Jack?'

I straightened up, wiped at the sweat running down my face and neck, looked at this little big man, and nodded.

I know now why they called him 'Blaster Bowen', and they couldn't really have called him anything else. He just blasted his way through life and applied the same principle to his job as a main-line driver.

He didn't just drive an engine. He pointed her in the direction he wanted her to go, gave her a well-aimed kick with a highly polished boot, cursed her, threatened her and slammed the regulator wide open to blast his way up any bank that dared to stand in his way.

On this trip I discovered that there was another side to Blaster Bowen. He knew what steam engines were all about. He respected his command of an awesome power and knew where this power came from and what made it work. Steam from the boilers, great drive-shafts pounding wheels ever onwards. He was at one with the engine and understood its needs, its strengths, its weaknesses.

He sympathised, gave her all the encouragement that he could, as well as guidance through the knowledge of his craft gained over the years as a top-link driver. I even

caught him talking to 8096 as she strained every nut and bolt to do his bidding. He even patted her boiler as though she were a dog eagerly trying to please.

He applied the same principles to his firemen. He expected the best they could give him and was unstinting in his praise for effort, but a hard taskmaster for the man wanting an easy ride.

But that night, as I stood on the heaving footplate of 8096, drenched in sweat with arms aching and fit to drop, back feeling as though it was broken in two like some stranded wreck on a reef, there was no great comfort to be gained from the great blasts Jock was giving on the whistle as we thundered onwards into the night.

Control were waiting on the side to see how far the mighty can fall, before moving in to scatter the pieces of the legend before the jackals of the envious and the weak.

Through Edwalton and Plumtree we sped with the staccato bark of 8096 reverberating

Ex-LMS 'Jubilee' Class 4-6-0 No 45605 *Cyprus* storming the 1 in 200 bank at Edwalton with a passenger train, the 1.15 Nottingham to St Pancras, on 12 April 1957. *Derek Murdoch*

Edwalton Station, circa 1955. *Douglas Thompson*

back at us from the surrounding hills. Into the great cavern of Stanton tunnel we thundered. I was firing continuously now and if this bloody pantomime continued for much longer it would be a forlorn gesture. Jock was getting rid of the fire quicker than I could get it on. Sweat rolled down my face and dripped on to the leaf-plate beneath my feet.

More coal, more fire. More fire, more coal. Shovel. Keep at it. Heat, steam, power. Keep the wheels turning, pulling.

Blaster on the whistle.

The wheels were beginning to back-skid under the sheer weight of the load, but we were still moving, winning.

Then the steep gradient and the heavy train began to take their toll. Our pace had slowed, and still three miles to go before we reached the top of the bank. Despite my efforts the pressure was dropping down from 225 lbs to 200 lbs. Jock looked across and motioned me to shut off the injector. I didn't want to as the gauge glass was only indicating half full and I was well aware that this was a false reading anyway due to the tilted-back attitude of the engine. However, Jock was the boss so off it went.

Messages were flashing between signal boxes and Control.

'He's definitely flagging. He's struggling!'

Tension was rising in Control. Bets were being placed. The Midland Division of the LMS Railway seemingly paused in its work of national importance.

Would they make it?

Meanwhile the two innocent participants were wrestling with the controls, pitting their wits against the near impossible. I speared more coal into the box, then more, and the pressure began to rise. Jock knocked off the valve gear - she'd now got the lot, everything. There was no more to give.

The level in the boiler was bobbing dangerously near the bottom of the glass in the yellow glare of the gauge lamp as the mouth of Grimston Tunnel closed agonisingly slowly around the labouring, straining boiler of 8096, but once through we would have mounted the bank. 8096 started to bark just that little bit louder. She was making a last great effort, every nut, bolt and rivet straining forward as the blast of wheels, fire and steam bounced off the grimy walls of the tunnel. With a further blast of triumph we inched our way clear of the embracing confines, wheels and couplings squealing. A final lurch, then our pace noticeably quickened. We were over the top.

We'd made it!

Jock half closed the regulator, I snapped on both injectors and watched fearfully for the water to reappear. 8096 began to blow off. She was telling the world 'I've made it! We've made it!'.

The water bobbed back into the glass. Jock shut down the regulator as we accelerated and with a wry grin said 'That was close, Jack. For a few minutes back there I thought we might have to call for a banker.'

My God, I thought. Control haven't got a bloody clue who they have taken on. Oh, they know the man by name and they know of his reputation, but they haven't seen him in action the way I have.

Jock Bowen was not just any five-foot-nothing driver, he was ten feet tall, every boy's dream of what a driver should be. Confident, professional, awe-inspiring. He could take on the world and beat it if he had a mind to.

Oh no, I shrugged, if Control are taking any bets in the future, no matter what the odds, my money will be going on Jock Bowen. Control stand as much chance of putting one over on Jock as a snowflake surviving in hell!

The signalman in Old Dalby flashed the news to Control as we thundered past him, Blaster Bowen on the whistle. And Control went back to normal. The LMS Railway heaved with a sigh of relief and got on with its job. The little 'Jockos' in the shunting yards gave a whoop of joy from their tinny whistles, and we rolled blithely on into Melton totally unaware of the trauma, the subterfuge, and the gnashing of teeth we had left in our wake.

The remainder of the trip was child's play in comparison, for the powers that be, realising that their 'get Bowen' plans had been scuppered, to their credit gave us the main line. This enabled us to drop down the water scoop over the troughs at Melton at speed, and within minutes we had caught 2,000 gallons, enough to see us into Wellingborough. This was a real boon as it saved us the trouble of stopping at the water crane and hauling the cumbersome bag across the tender.

Through Whissendine, then Oakham and Manton Tunnel. Next the gloriously arched Harringworth Viaduct, 275 yards in length on 82 arches. 8096 dipped her nose into the valley then quickened her pace to breast the rise. Half regulator and notched up 20 per cent was all she needed to hustle the 700-ton train along at a cracking pace.

And what a treat it was to fire such a smooth-running engine. No piston valves blowing and no continuous thump from worn axle boxes. We decided to enjoy it while it lasted, for with the day-by-day pounding these engines received it would not be long before she was back to her old bone-shaking ways. A dozen shovels around the firebox every five minutes soon had her safety valves popping - she was a real beauty was old 8096. And Jock was in his element, singing away at the top of his voice with just the occasional grin in my direction, giving me the thumbs up.

The miles simply flew by and the blinding white flashes of the blast furnaces at Corby piercing the night sky next came into view, before drastically being cut of by the one-mile-long Corby tunnel. Jock eased off the regulator and allowed the train to slow down for the curve at Glendon Junction, where we joined the main London to Leicester line. Through Kettering Station and our destination was soon in sight - Finedon Road signal box, where the relief Wellingborough driver and fireman stood waiting to carry our train onwards to Brent.

Hardly a word had passed between Jock and myself, so exhilarating had been the trip. But it was with a sigh of tired relief that we relinquished our sturdy steed and set off to sample the dubious delights of the railway lodge, me with my haversack and billy-can, and Jock with his tin trunk in one hand and trusty block of wood in the other. After a wash and brush up, followed by a hearty breakfast, we knew no more until rudely awakened by one of the staff at dinner time. Then it was out on the town for a couple of well-deserved pints before signing on at 6 pm for our return journey.

Another Class '8' awaited us at Finedon

Road with a Wellingborough crew in charge, No 8027, coupled up to 60 empty wagons, non-stop back to Kirkby. No problem here - 8027 hustled them along contemptuously. The only slight difficulty we would encounter would be the ten-mile-long steep bank that lay between Nottingham and Kirkby, but she stormed up it, and breasted Annesley Tunnel as though she knew she was on home ground. She wanted to be fed, watered and have a rest - didn't we all?

To his credit, Jock insisted on seeking my father out. When he found him he said 'You've no need to worry about this lad, Darky. I'll take him with me any time.'

Praise indeed from such a magnificent engineman as Jock Bowen. But quite seriously, one trip a month with the fearsome Blaster Bowen was enough for me; I think I slept for a week.

As far as I was concerned Jock and Control could play their game of cat and mouse with another unsuspecting pawn. Just for a little while I intended having a Grandmother hovering at death's door!

I was also booked on the Burton-on-Trent run many times. Being the beer capital of the Midlands, we used to relish this job for we always had an interesting night out on the town after signing off. They were similar trains to the Wellingborough run in that we would again lodge and work home the following day.

I remember one such trip particularly because we worked home one of the mighty 2-6-0+0-6-2 Beyer Garratts. These were enormous engines with two water tenders and four cylinders, ideal engines for heavy long-distance work. They were housed mainly at Toton for the London runs, and from my single experience of working on one they were more than welcome to them - not a patch on our more modern Class '8s'.

But a run to Wakefield in South Yorkshire one day really put into perspective the importance of being prepared for all emergencies, particularly the importance of taking enough food and provisions to last the trip out.

I had brought sufficient food to see me through a normal eight-hour shift, knowing full well that we would be relieved and lodge at Wakefield. But the Kirkby driver, wise man that he was, and with whom I was booked for the two days' work, came supplied, as usual, with what can be best described as a food hamper instead of the usual haversack.

We were booked as express freight and had a clear line all the way into Yorkshire where we were due to shunt in and out of three collieries *en route*. Our destination then lay over branch lines, in some cases single track, which necessitated exchanging tablets at each signal box. This invariably caused delays if traffic happened to be coming from the opposite direction, causing us to await the other train's arrival for its driver to relinquish his single-line 'tablet'. This would then be passed to us

Beyer Garratt No 47999, with fixed bunker, at Toton MPD (18A) in May 1954. *Derek Murdoch*

Two views of Beyer Garratt No 47981 with revolving, self-trimming tender at Toton MPD (18A) in August 1956. Despite their size they weren't a patch on our Class '8' 2-8-0s. *Derek Murdoch*

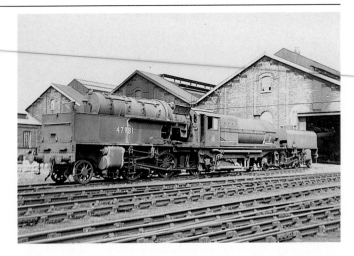

to allow us to proceed a further stage forward. All these delays quickly added up to the point at which we had only half covered our journey when the eight hours had elapsed!

I had long since polished off the food that I'd taken with me and was beginning to feel very hungry and thirsty. The Kirkby driver soon remedied this by unpacking his hamper, complete with a full set of cutlery. And, by gum, what a feast we had.

Bread, butter and cheese with a couple of onions that had been roasting away over the hot injector pipe ever since we had fortunately been stopped a few miles back right next to a large field full of them; they couldn't have placed a signal in a better spot. And as we were able to fill our billy-cans at any signal box or station, we were mashing all the way into Wakefield, which we eventually reached after spending eighteen hours on the footplate! I was never to be caught out again, for if any trip looked like taking longer than normal, I made sure I was well prepared.

I always enjoyed these trips out of Kirkby loco, for although the majority of drivers were strangers to me, the first person I would seek out after signing on at the time office would be my father if he happened to be on the same shift as myself. More often than not I would find him as he seemed to spend more time at work than he did at home during the war years. I'm sure my mother used to think there was another woman involved, but, like most railwaymen, he had neither the time nor the energy. You were quite simply married to the job. You only had to ask anyone 'Have you seen Darky?', and they would readily tell you where to find him, usually on one engine or another. Having found him, he would quickly put me at my ease by introducing me to the relevant driver of the day, making my job just that little bit easier.

6
ROUNDING UP THE STRAYS

Meanwhile, back at my home loco I was rapidly nearing being booked into a passenger link. This meant that I would be spending the next year with different drivers in rotation in what was then a ten-week cycle comprising 5 am and 5 pm shifts. As matters turned out it would be another nine or ten months before this happened. In many ways the type of work that came my way in those preceding months turned out to be much more interesting, if only for its diversity, for I found myself with a new driver on a different route most days of the week.

I still hadn't any consistent main-line experience as yet - this would only happen when I entered a passenger link on a permanent basis because in reality we were all technically probationers for the first two years of firing.

Quite a large proportion of the firing duties I found myself engaged on were delivering stray engines to their home depots, then travelling back passenger, or vice versa. This was a comparatively easy job as well as being very interesting except for the fact that one or two alarming incidents occurred during the collections that only went to prove that you daren't take it easy or relax your vigil, even on the most simple day's work.

For instance, take the day Bill Morris, my driver, and myself, together with a registered fireman named Jimmy Clay, were sent passenger to Wellingborough. Our task was to drive back to Mansfield two engines that had strayed from the fold. The plan was for Bill and myself to man the leading Class '8' engine, which of course would be live and in steam, and we would tow the second Class '4'

engine which, in theory, was supposed to be dead, that is with no fire or steam.

However, being December and a very cold day, Jim decided to build up the fire which had been left to die out on the Class '4' to provide him with a little warmth on the long trip home. This was strictly against the rules which stated that if an engine was in steam, even if only 40 pounds per square inch, it must not be moved unless manned by a full crew. Within the following two hours it turned out to be very fortuitous for us that Jimmy had decided to bend the rules.

It was another rule that one of a fireman's many duties before taking an engine off the Loco was to test both injectors to make certain that they worked properly, these being the most vital parts of equipment on the footplate. But, as in all walks of life, rules, as they say, are designed to be bent a little, and this proved to be no exception, for in all my years on the railway I never saw a fireman test them both. The procedure was to flip one on and listen for the singing note that told the fireman instantly that all was well. He'd then switch it off and proceed with the other many and varied duties that were a fireman's lot. The only exception we used to make to this life-long habit was if we were due to go on a long hard haul where we were likely to need both injectors on at the same time; in such circumstances both would be tested individually.

As this was a line I hadn't travelled along very much in the past I decided to put a good stoke on to allow myself as much opportunity as possible to view the places of interest and learn the road at the same time. We hooked

Ex-LMS Class '4' 0-6-0 No 44425 at Kirkby MPD in August 1955, similar to the one we retrieved from Wellingborough. *Derek Murdoch*

Ex-LMS Class '4' 0-6-0 No 44425 at Kirkby MPD in August 1955, similar to the one we retrieved from Wellingborough. *Derek Murdoch*

up to Jim's engine and, the signals showing clear for the goods line, away we went. All was well for the first ten miles, which had taken us through Kettering, when, with the boiler showing half full, I decided to switch on the injector on my side of the engine to top her up.

It didn't work. All that was happening was that the steam and water that should have combined to form a jet and force its way into the boiler was spilling out of the overflow pipe on to the ballast on the track below. No matter how I tried, it was useless. By now the boiler was down to only a quarter full. But no matter, I shrugged. We've still got the injector on the driver's side. I nipped across and switched that one on, and that too proved utterly useless!

We now found ourselves in a position that should never have arisen. Whenever an engine was taken on to a Loco after a hard day's work, it was the driver's unfailing duty to fill out a report card detailing any malfunction regarding the working controls. No matter how trivial the malfunction, the report had to be made, and believe me the injectors were anything but trivial, for without them you were totally lost. Under the circumstances we could only assume that for some unknown reason the normal procedure had not been carried out, but this was cold comfort to us in our present predicament.

We had an engine with about half a ton of white-hot fire in its belly, and a boiler with the water level so low that it had practically disappeared out of sight at the bottom of the gauge glass! Being on a busy line and between signal boxes at the time, there was no siding where we could be turned off, thus clearing the way for following traffic. We had no option but to carry on to Glendon Junction four miles off and hope to get there before the water in the boiler dropped below the level of the two lead-filled plugs in the crown of the firebox. If that happened, appalling consequences would surely follow.

The ten minutes it took us to reach Glendon Junction were the longest ten minutes of my life. We kept alternately turning on the injectors, hoping against hope, but they remained useless. We'd really got the wind up by this time, for the remaining water was almost non-existent. We simply stood there listening for the sudden roar from the firebox that would signify that the plugs had blown. Although there was a safety margin built into the system, we had long since passed it and were now living on pure luck. I had already closed the dampers and opened the firebox doors to try and dissipate the heat being generated by the fire, but the only effect this had was to knock back the steam pressure to 150 pounds. I daren't go any lower.

At long last Glendon Junction came into sight and we pulled up bang outside the signal box. The 'bobby' opened his window and we breathlessly informed him of our desper-

'At last Glendon Junction came into sight. . .' '8F' No 48266 approaches Glendon South Junction on the down goods lines from Kettering with a Cardiff-Corby coal train in September 1964. The main line continues to the left towards Glendon North Junction and Leicester, while the Corby and Manton Junction line curves away to the right. *Robin J. Cullup*

ate predicament. He immediately switched us into the siding at the side of his box in order to keep the main line free. But we knew damn well that there would not be sufficient time left to lift the fire manually, for in the first place it was too flaming hot, and in the second place there wasn't flaming time. There was just too much of it. We had already decided that the only course open to us was to force the straight dart, one of our fire-irons ten feet in length and shaped like a dart at its tip, between the fire bars then twist and hope we could pull two or three clear of the rack.

Once more Lady Luck was on our side, for two of them popped out, providing us with just enough space to thrust the fire through into the ashpan with the long shovel provided. I clambered down on to the track armed with the hosepipe that all engines carried for

just such an emergency, and tried to douse the fire as Bill pushed it through. Even so, the sleepers were beginning to catch alight. To put it shortly, we were in a right bloody mess! But we had to save the engine at all costs. How on earth we succeeded I'll never know.

Whilst we were busily engaged in our rescue operation Jim, on the second engine, knew what was happening. He was frantically trying to build up the fire on his Class '4' to get sufficient steam pressure to enable us to reverse the positions of the two engines. This would provide us with the means of continuing our journey with as little delay as possible, and get us off the bloody hook at the same time!

But this was going to be a very tricky operation, as we had very little time in which to complete it.

By now we had finished drawing the fire in the Class '8' and the steam pressure was dropping rapidly. We also had no alternative but to change the engines round under their own steam. We daren't call for assistance for this manoeuvre as we were in enough trouble already without making matters any worse. I just managed to salvage five or six shovels of fire before it finally died out under the engine and passed them up to Jim to help him build up his - the operation was turning into a race against time. Pressure was rapidly dropping on the '8', and the '4' did not, as yet, have enough steam pressure to produce the power needed to turn the wheels.

It took another 45 minutes of coaxing, cajoling and cursing before the Class '4' began to show signs of life. The fire roared away merrily now that there was sufficient pressure to operate the blower valve, and the needle on the gauge had risen to 60 pounds per square inch. This would give us just enough power to turn the wheels, but not enough to work the brakes. Fortunately, being on a level stretch, we would be able to stop her if necessary by screwing on the hand brake.

Having got the OK from the 'bobby', we ran the Class '8' out of the siding and reversed down the main line far enough to clear the points. Jim then drove the Class '4' out, passed us and reversed on to our engine. I coupled up and we exchanged engines with Jim who was then in charge of the by now dead Class '8' and, despite his efforts, he was still in for a cold ride home. But how fortunate it turned out for us that all this was what he had been trying to avoid in the first place!

The rest of the journey back proved to be very hard work, for now we were towing the giant Class '8', which was 120 tons dead weight, and any steep uphill gradients that we encountered pulled us right back. Nevertheless we eventually made it home and, having inspected the firebox on the Class '8' and found to our profound relief that it was OK, the mission was completed, but not without its fair share of apprehension, excitement and hard graft.

Another memorable trip that still lives vividly in my mind occurred one day when three sets of men were sent from Mansfield to Peterborough to return three more of our engines that had strayed from the fold. This was becoming an all too prevalent occurrence due solely to the effect the war was having on all rolling-stock. We were rapidly reaching the position where the traffic would be at point A and the engines that were supposed to convey that traffic would be at point B. The result of this would have been sheer chaos if allowed to continue, hence all the chasing around to put matters right.

I was booked with a driver named Fred Thomas. We all piled into our local train to Nottingham where we picked up the London express as far as Manton and there changed for Peterborough. We made ourselves known to the time office from where we were directed to the bay in which our three engines were waiting for us. We tossed a coin to see who would take the leading engine, and we lost, making my driver responsible for all the signals whilst the other two sets of men could sit back and take it easy. Fred elected to take one of the two Class '8s' with a Class '4' bringing up the rear. We coupled up, got the right of way from the 'bobby' and off we set.

After covering about half of the run to Manton, in the distance off to our left we spotted the distinctive red coats of the local hunt approaching us across an open field. As they rapidly drew nearer to us we could just make out the pack of baying hounds about 200 yards in front of the riders. Fifty yards in front of the hounds was a fox running for its life. In our opinion there was no way he was going to make it.

Naturally, being townies, and therefore animal lovers, we were all shouting like hell for the fox while at the same time shaking our clenched fists at the riders. I have often heard the saying 'As cunning as an old fox', but had never seen any evidence to support it. However, little did we realise at the time that we were about to become privileged spectators to witness it at first hand.

The hunt was now 300 yards away from our cavalcade of engines, and the fox was approaching at such an angle that his quivering nose was pointing directly towards our lead engine, almost as though bent on committing suicide.

But not Reynard. He'd got quite a bit of living to do yet and was about to prove it. When he was about 15 yards away from us, with the teeth of the hounds snapping at his tail only a further ten yards behind, he cleared the boundary fence in one mighty leap and, gauging his run to the inch, flew across the front buffers of our engine. He was so close we feared we must have run him over, but, dashing over to the other side of the engine, there he was running for all his worth across the field after having cleared the second fence in the same fashion that he had surmounted the first. And I could have sworn there was a sly grin on his face!

The hounds had been nowhere near as lucky. The old fox had known precisely what he had been planning and he'd sprung the trap beautifully with his well-timed run, leaving just enough space to clear us. But the dogs, clearly having but one thought in their minds and completely unaware of the terrible danger in which they'd placed themselves, ran headlong under the churning wheels of our three engines. I've no idea how many we actually ran over. All I know is that you can't argue with engines weighing 120 tons each, and win.

The last we were to see of this happy or sad occasion, depending upon your point of view, were the irate huntsmen shaking their fists furiously at us in return.

7
A FRIGHTENING EXPERIENCE

One of the main reasons I was not in any particular hurry to be booked into a regular passenger link was purely financial. By this time, 1943, I had been firing consistently for two years and had amassed a considerable amount of experience, and this experience enabled me to be booked on quite a few main-line and long-distance jobs. As this often meant lodging away one night and then working back the following day, I was managing to clock up a considerable amount of overtime. I would often be taking home more in my pay packet than even the top-link drivers!

It gave me a great deal of pleasure to be able to pass this extra money to my mother, for although my father had always been in regular work his pay was rigidly set at £2 8s per week during the 'twenties and 'thirties when they were struggling to bring up my sister and myself. This never allowed for any extras and times must have been very difficult for them.

I vividly remember the first such occasion that I was to take home my extra wages. Having worked 28 hours of overtime, plus night rate, the sum total amounted to £12, a veritable fortune in those days. I handed the twelve crisp new notes over to my mother as she sat in the chair. She looked at them in utter bewilderment, momentarily not knowing what to do or say. At that time I didn't understand why, but in retrospect I now realise that for the first time in a great number of years she had a sum of money in her hand that was not already earmarked to pay off something or someone. For a little while this confused her, bless her! The old saying

that it's better to give than receive really is true, you know!

But alongside happy occasions, sad ones, alas, are never far away. I was made aware of this quite vividly one morning as I was cycling home after a hard night's work. It also served to remind me of how extremely fortunate I was to not only pursue my chosen profession, but also be able to enjoy life itself. My home lay a couple of miles distant from the Loco and it was my habit to use the cycle path through Titchfield Park.

On this particular day there was a gang of council workmen repairing the footpath and I had to dismount to go round them. The first man in the gang I encountered seemed

My mother, Marie Backen, on holiday at Southsea in 1957. *Author*

to be leaning disconsolately on his shovel. On looking closer I immediately recognised him to be the father of my old pal, Alan Penford, who had tried to join with me as a fireman two years previously.

'Good morning, Mr Penford,' I greeted him. 'How are you keeping?'

He looked up at me. His face was tired, haggard almost, through having had to bear its fair share of life's burdens. He didn't answer.

'Remember me?' I queried. 'Jack Backen - your son Alan's friend. By the way, how is he? I haven't heard from him lately.'

His voice trembled as he answered 'Nor will you, lad - ever again.'

The surprise must have been evident on my face for he motioned me to one side out of earshot of his mates. His head dropped, his shoulders trembled.

'What is it, Mr Penford?' I asked gently, for even my young years could sense tragedy; sometimes words weren't necessary.

Tears were slowly running down his face, and to see at first hand these visible signs of distress pouring unashamedly from a strong hard-bitten man such as him was devastating. But having precipitated this encounter by my innocent yet seemingly clumsy questions, I knew in my heart that it was better for all concerned to pursue the encounter further, not so much for my sake but for his - we had gone too far for me to turn my back on him. His voice was hollow.

'We received a telegram this morning from the War Office. It didn't say very much,' he said bitterly. 'I would imagine there were less words in the message than years Alan had lived!'

I didn't believe what I thought I'd heard him say. I caught my breath.

'Had? *Had* lived?'

His eyes welled more tears. Sadly, he shook his head.

'Yes, you heard me right, *had* lived. You see, lad, the telegram informed his mother and me that he's been killed in action.'

I just looked at him, not knowing what to say, so I said nothing. It was not for me to intrude on his private grief.

He sighed heavily, and looked up at me.

'I had to get out. I thought I'd be better off at work with my mates. Take my mind off it a little bit. . .'

I left him with his memories, a sad, forlorn figure of a man. I knew, as I'm certain he knew if he searched his heart, however well intentioned his reasons had been at the time, that he had unwittingly become one of the prime instruments of his own son's fate.

Tears were running down my own face as I thought of the events that had taken place two years ago, of Alan's earnest desire to team up with me to continue our friendship; his excitement at being accepted into the railway industry had mirrored my own. I remembered also his great disappointment on learning that his father had blocked the move, his words being '. . .that he didn't see the railway as a very rewarding life for a young man'.

So instead Alan had to go off to fight a war.

'My God,' I thought, 'that poor man must be going through hell!'

I was to learn, years later, the sad truth about Alan's death. His regiment, the Royal Marines, had been in the forefront of the action during the Allied attack on the Salerno beaches just below Naples in Italy. The landings, undertaken by the US 5th Army and the British 10th, ran into stiff enemy opposition from well-sited dug-in machine-gun posts and from mobile artillery batteries supported by tanks from the 16th Panzer Division. On 13 September 1943 the German counter-attack was halted by heavy naval bombardment, and on the 16th the Allies broke out from Salerno and joined with Montgomery's 8th Army. During the fighting and the sheer hell and carnage that is the real face of war, more than 25,000 men were killed or wounded at Salerno. Alan was one of them.

I have never forgotten him - and I never will.

We had a frightening experience one night as we were piloting a Toton-bound coal train from Shirebrook. These trains were usually double-headed because they not only needed the extra pulling power up the bank as far as Kirkby, but also needed the extra braking that a second engine could provide on the very steep descent down to Pye Bridge. These heavy coal trains could soon run away completely out of control if you didn't keep a tight check on them. The usual drill then would be to unhook and bank an empty wagon train back up the hill.

We briskly got the train under way out of Shirebrook Sidings and approached Sutton Junction where there was a set of 'Jack points' that closed shut as you ran over them, but snapped back open again as soon as you cleared them to catch and derail any part of a train that broke away and ran backwards; consequently you always made absolutely certain that you were hopping along at a fair pace as you clicked over them.

On this particular occasion it was indeed fortunate that we had the train well under way, with a little to spare. As we passed the spot where the old hide and skin warehouse used to stand until a week previously, when it had been demolished, we passed over the 'Jack points' and our engine, in company with the train engine behind us, started to slip very badly and, unexpectedly, seeing as we were running on a dry line, Tom, my driver, snapped on the steam sands - we had to maintain traction.

The sanders made little difference. It was dark at the time but there was a full moon and we were both leaning over the side of the engine to try and see what was causing us all the trouble. At first all we could see was what seemed to be a moving grey mass. As our eyes became more accustomed to the faint light given off by the moon we were surprised and horrified at the incredible spectacle that faced us.

Rats! Hundreds of thousands of them, it seemed. A swarm of biblical proportions, 12 yards wide - and we could see neither the front nor the end of it! A great heaving grey mass of fur and teeth lathering and snarling its way from what must have been the site of the old hide and skin warehouse, over the tracks like a moving grey carpet and, judging by the way the engines were behaving, we must have been running over scores of them!

We were very thankful that we were ten feet above them with the solid steel of the footplate between us, but even now I shudder to think of the consequences had we been caught in their path on foot.

Nevertheless our immediate worry was that we were now rapidly beginning to lose momentum due to loss of wheel traction and were in imminent danger of slipping to a complete halt. If this were to happen, the sheer weight of the train would pull us backwards and off the 'Jack points', and there was damn all we could do about it.

And out there were the rats.

Although we were safe whilst we were on the move, I would not have liked to predict the outcome if we had come to a standstill, victim to murine rodents on the rampage. There would have been no stopping them. They would have climbed over everything and everybody and the mere thought of what might happen filled us with horror.

I often heard stories of rats leaving a sinking ship or the condemned slaughter house, migrating in swarms, devouring all in front of them, but I never thought I would live to see the day when I would actually experience the sight at first hand. It was a terrifying incident and one I hope never to see again.

Fortunately for us, the steam sanders on our engines began to bite and take effect and we gradually began to regain traction. It seemed agonisingly slow, but having almost come to a complete stop we were beginning to inch our way forward and out of danger from both the rats and the 'Jack points'.

It became quite a talking point at the Loco for weeks afterwards, but from a personal point of view it was best forgotten. It used to give me nightmares every time the subject was mentioned.

8
BLOWING OFF STEAM

June the second 1943 was a rather special day in my life. It was the birthday of the young lady to whom I was engaged, but that day remains in my memory for a very different reason.

We had planned a night out on the town as a celebration, and as I was due to sign on at ten o'clock in the morning for shed duties only, and could therefore guarantee being back home by six, no problem, I thought. But a knock on the door at eight o'clock that same morning prompted the first indication that it was to be no ordinary day. The caller was a junior cleaner from the Loco.

I was to sign on at twelve mid-day, then catch the passenger train to Kirkby.

'Don't know what's in the wind, Jack,' the youngster said, 'but you're the third fireman I've visited with the same message. The other two knocked off sick. I can't understand it, they looked OK to me. All I told them is what I've told you. Oh, and I did happen to mention that Jock Bowen would be their driver.'

Below 'Courting innocents abroad.' Myself and my wife-to-be, Maisie, in August 1941. *Author*

Right Maisie, in another 1941 portrait. *Author*

I burst out laughing. 'Oh, I can well understand them knocking off sick. Blaster Bowen, eh?'

'Yes, shouldn't I have mentioned it?' he asked hesitantly.

'I'll bet you weren't supposed to!'

'Oh Lord.' His face dropped. Then, by way of explanation, he said, 'I was in the office, you see, when the information came through and I overheard the time-keeper repeat his name. . .'

'That's OK, I'll say nothing. Tell them I'll be there by twelve.'

I was comforted by the thought that this was quite evidently not a lodging job. One day with Blaster Bowen I could stand, but two was asking a bit much. Yet, having said that, when you were Jock's fireman you crammed two and a half days firing into one anyway.

This was to be no exception.

I discovered him in the messroom, after having paid my usual visit to the fitters shop to say hello to my dad. I tapped him on the shoulder.

'I'm your fireman. Remember me, Darky's son?'

'Sure I do,' he grinned. 'Have you recovered from the Wellingborough trip yet? Your dad told me you slept for a week.'

I cautioned myself before answering - you took Jock for granted at your peril.

'I'm fine, Jock, thank you. Dad exaggerates a bit now and then. What run are we on today?'

He grasped my shoulder and led me out of earshot, a devilish grin spreading across his face.

'Oh, God,' I thought, 'not another cat and mouse game between him and Control'.

Outside the messroom he cast a furtive glance up and down, then whispered secretly, 'There's a bit of a flap on, and just between you and me it looks like Control have made a right bloody cock-up. You see, there's 170 wagons of coal in Shirebrook sidings that shouldn't be there. They should be here, in Kirkby. They're urgently needed to make up three block trains to Brent. They're due out at seven o'clock tonight. The powers that be have already cleared a through path for them

between passenger trains, and there'll be hell to pay if they miss their slot!'

I looked at him in silence. He went on.

'But there you are, that's Control for you. They think they've got their fingers on the pulse,' he snorted, 'but they couldn't run a brothel in Soho without getting their knickers in a twist. The silly buggers would have the tarts paying the customers!'

His five-foot-nothing frame started to quiver. Everything started to quiver. His fierce moustache, penetrating blue eyes, even his trusty block of wood tucked beneath his arm started to quiver as he rasped 'But do you know what's really made me mad, Jack? The cheeky buggers had the temerity to suggest that I could have a pilot engine hooked up on to the front of us if I needed helping out.'

'ME!' he literally shouted. 'ME. . .Jock Bowen, a pilot engine? I've never been so bloody insulted in all my life! There's only 170 blasted wagons,' he spat, 'and they've cleared the line for us between passengers to do it in three drifts. So I told them, Jack. I told them in no uncertain terms where they could stuff their bloody pilot engine!'

'But Jock. . .' I started to say, before thinking better of it and keeping my opinion to myself. Strictly speaking Jock was right. The maximum load for a Class '8' freight engine from Shirebrook to Kirkby was 57 wagons, therefore in three drifts we would have cleared them. But as I have said before, never in my limited experience was any engine loaded down to the maximum. It was universally considered impossible. I must have fired on a hundred trips out of Shirebrook on this same run, but always the guard knocked off at least half a dozen wagons. Even then, unless everything was spot on, such as a damned good engine, a dry line, a clear road through to your destination and an experienced crew, I'd had more than my share of heart-stopping moments.

The distance in question was no more than twelve miles, mostly uphill, but the most notorious spot was centred between Woodhouse and Mansfield, six miles up the line. It was so heavy there that the railway hierarchy had installed a set of 'Jack points' in case a coupling broke. What was more relevant in this particular case as far as we were concerned was that we were so overloaded we could lose our forward impetus, come to an abrupt halt, then start to slide backwards and be de-railed. We were faced, therefore, with not just the problem of taking one fully loaded train through these 'Jack points', but three on the trot. I was mulling over what lay ahead with a familiar dryness at the back of my throat when I noticed Jock looking quizzically into my face.

'You were about to say, Jack?'

I thought of the other two firemen who had reported in sick.

'Oh, nothing of any importance, Jock.'

To turn his attention away from me I asked, 'What engine have they given us?' He tapped the destination board.

'I'll say this for them, they've given us a good 'un. 8033. She's new out of the shops.'

He was still muttering under his breath as we strolled across to number four bay to pick her up.

'Bloody pilot engine. . . They know where they can shove it!'

Initially I couldn't for the life of me understand why Jock wanted to take this job on unassisted, for in normal times he'd see them in hell first before even condescending to do them a favour. But as I watched him bustling around on his trusty steed I began to understand. They had piqued his pride. They had committed the cardinal sin, in his eyes, of casting doubt on his ability.

I just wonder, I mused; have they set him up again as a fall guy? Even Control, in their cosy little office where the hardest manual work undertaken was the sharpening of a pencil, must realise that they are asking the near impossible.

That they were in a mess was indisputable. But however much of a mess they found themselves in, I once again wouldn't have put it past them to use it as an excuse to institute a trial of strength between their force of twelve or thirteen black-suited bowler-hatted miniature 'Gods', with all the awesome power they commanded at the touch of a button in their own little corner, and tiny, unsuspecting Jock Bowen in the other.

It was as though they were gathering around Dionysius, and Jock Bowen was to be their Damocles. But it would not be the sword hanging by a hair that would fall upon his head if he faltered, but the 2,000 tons of coal needed at Kirkby.

Jock shook me out of my reverie by crashing his block of wood down on to the floorboards of 8033. Up he leapt to blast away on the hooter for the 'bobby' to turn us out main line.

Off we flew, and the game had begun.

The word must have got around. It was 'High Noon' again, and there was quite a gathering to see us depart from the old corral. Hands were dipping into pockets. I wondered what kind of bets were being laid - and what kind of odds.

Out we shot, accompanied by a hail from the signalman.

'You've got ten minutes before the passenger's on your tail, Jock.'

'That'll do.'

We slowed down as we passed the up sidings to pick up our guard, then went hell for leather down the bank to Shirebrook. I could just hear their conversation as I started to build up the fire. This was the number one priority for me, to get it white hot before the slog began.

'Think we can do it, Jock?' Ernie Bristow, our guard, asked tremulously.

'Don't be bloody silly!' Jock rasped.

'You could have another engine hooked on front. . .' Ernie began to explain before being stopped by a red-faced Jock.

'Another engine? What the hell would I want another engine for? There's only 171 wagons! Three full loads! What the hell's wrong with them in Control, can't they bloody well count?'

'I know, but. . .'

'No bloody buts. . .' Jock shut him up. 'We'll bloody do it!'

Within fifteen minutes we were switching through the points that led us into Shirebrook loaded sidings.

'I'll just nip round them to make sure they're all coupled and the brakes off,' Ernie said. He was back in no time and glancing at his watch shouted up, 'Two o'clock now.

They're turning us straight out after the 2.20 passenger, Jock.'

'Righto. Now listen, Ernie, nip up to the signal box and tell the bobby we want the road. We're stopping for nothing and no one between here and Kirkby. Understand?'

Ernie nodded eagerly. 'Leave it to me.'

He came back on the run, jumped up on to the footplate and gasped 'Control's already been on to him. They've given him strict instructions not to turn you out until he can guarantee you a clear line.'

'Hmm,' Jock condescended, 'they've got a bit more sense than I gave them credit for.' He turned to me. 'How are you doing Jack? We've got ten minutes.'

I slammed more coal into the firebox, paused to straighten up and said 'I'll be ready, Jock.'

'Good lad,' he bristled. 'Once we set off it'll be all hands to the pumps. We daren't hang about.'

A shrill whistle from the main line caused me to cease my labours and I gave an answering whistle to one of my mates from Mansfield Loco, Walt Haynes, as he hustled the passenger train through. I could do no more as far as preparation was concerned for what lay ahead of us. A boiler full of water, blowing off through both safety cocks, and a ton of white-hot fire roaring away in the belly of the 12-foot-long firebox.

The red stop signal to turn us out main line flew off. The steam sanders went on to give our driving wheels grip and forward went the lever to shut off the cylinder drain taps. The reversing gear went right down, regulator hard across. No gentle easing out of the couplings on this massive load. Stretching them quickly would give us the flying start we desperately needed before the full weight descended on us.

No 8033 leapt ahead like a greyhound released from its trap and stormed out of the sidings. The first couple of miles along the slight uphill gradient, then the one mile straight through Woodhouse, allowed us just enough margin to get them really on the trot. Jock had deliberately left the regulator fully open but had notched up the reversing gear a couple of turns. We hit the start of the bank, two miles short of Mansfield, at about 20 miles per hour, but as soon as she started to falter under the tremendous weight strung out behind her, Jock released the clip on the reversing lever allowing it to fly down to maximum power.

And my God, what thunder!

One mile into the bank the line crossed over a main road, then began to cross the impressive stone viaduct that carries the track over bustling Mansfield. As we blasted our way over the top of the town all the bustling ceased. Everything - cars, buses, pedestrians. Eyes turned to the sky to discover why Mansfield was shaking.

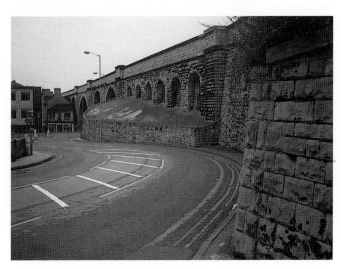

'As we blasted our way over the top of the town all the bustling ceased.' Mansfield viaduct in 1990. *Author*

An '8F' in full cry - No 48225 gets to grips with an up mineral train on the climb to Sharnbrook, on the Midland Main Line, in November 1965. *K. C. H. Fairey*

The exhaust was deafening. The great steel-track-bound Leviathan that was 8033, with its dragon's tail of fifty-seven wagons, really turned it on for the watching audience. There was a great 'Whoosh' as she popped her safety valves.

Then she started to slip.

'Stop that, you silly bugger. . .!' Jock yelled at her as he snapped on the sands and wrestled with the controls. '. . .there's a good lass.'

He spoke softly as she dug her heels in. 'Come on, my beauty, you can do it.'

I watched, and thought damn me, he's talking to her - and I'm damned sure she understands him!

What an engineman. What a master. What a motivator. Man and machine were one as he coaxed, cajoled, even threatened all in the same breath.

Yet even under his watchful eye our pace had faltered to 10 miles per hour. I was firing as rapidly and as skilfully as I knew how just to keep the pressure up.

Seven miles an hour, still 300 yards to go. 'Pop' went the safety valves again. 8033 was striving might and main, driven on by this superb driver. Again her mighty frame began to judder towards a slip.

'No you don't, my old beauty,' Jock breathed, giving her a whiff of sand beneath her eight massive driving wheels.

She recovered.

'There's a good lass.' He flashed a grin at me from his sweat-streaked face, then gave 8033 a friendly pat on her sizzling boiler.

Five miles an hour.

As I looked back the guard's brake had cleared the 'Jack points', but one more slip from 8033 and all would be lost.

No chance. She daren't. Blaster Bowen was in charge. I think she'd have sooner died than disobey him.

We crawled into the confines of Mansfield Station, the blast from our twin cylinders almost tearing holes in the protective check-plates above our heads. But no doubt about it, she was barking that little bit faster now. Jock gave me a wicked little grin and the thumbs-up.

'I'll bet the silly buggers thought we couldn't do it,' he yelled at me triumphantly.

I was too busy to reply - we still had six miles to cover. But they were a picnic compared to the last six. Oh, she still needed all that Jock and I could give her, but she wasn't going to falter now.

Two miles up from the station we ran past my home Loco. There was quite a turn-out as we thundered by - they were waving caps and urging us on. Jock gave them a series of hoots from the whistle to let them know, even then, that there was only one 'Blaster Bowen'.

He was in his element, singing 'Oh, the runaway train went down the track as she blew' at the top of his voice. He jumped on to his trusty block of wood and vigorously polished the glasses of the vacuum and steam gauges. 'Might as well clean your face for you lass.' Giving her shuddering frame a friendly pat, he grinned 'There's a good girl.'

Personally I'd never heard a 120-ton monster purr, but I'm sure I did that day. I honestly believe that if she'd been able to curtsey she would have, for Jock.

On through Sutton Station and our goal was in sight, the signal showing clear to turn us into Kirkby sidings. There was no need to announce our arrival - they'd heard us pounding up the track three miles distant.

Amongst the reception committee we spotted the distant figure of an Inspector, sent hot-foot by control to supervise and direct the operations. No sooner had our wheels stopped turning when he jumped aboard. These men had the power to intimidate you with a single withering glance, and six-foot-three Inspector Branston was the most intimidating of the bunch.

But not on Jock Bowen's footplate. He was master in his own domain and when an Inspector came aboard the intimidating boot was on the other foot.

Branston was already on the defensive. 'No problems, driver?' he asked solicitously.

'Problems?' Jock snorted. 'Why the hell should we have problems?'

The portly Inspector then committed the cardinal sin of removing his LMS Railway-issue bowler hat. Jock, immediately seizing the initiative, jumped up on to his trusty block of wood, thus raising himself to the exalted height of five foot nine. The sum total of this manoeuvre meant that instead of Jock talking to Inspector Branston's railway-issue waistcoat, he was looking directly into his railway-issue smoke-stained moustache, making them almost level-pegging. But only as far as height was concerned. Jock was yards higher in confidence and authority. He swivelled in my direction.

'We've had no problems have we Jack?'

'None that we couldn't overcome,' I trembled. I was not imbued with Jock's fearlessness in the company of such an exalted personage as the dreaded Inspector Branston.

'Nevertheless, driver,' the Inspector mumbled, 'you did a fine job back there.'

I almost burst into uncontrollable laughter at the sight of him standing in the full glare of the roaring fire with his bowler hat placed elegantly across his chest. He had taken on the appearance of an out-of-work funeral director. One contemptuous glance from him soon wiped the smirk off my face - he still represented God in my eyes. But not in Jock's. I doubt if he would even have rated as a novice pall-bearer to him.

'We're only doing the job we're paid to do,' he rasped. 'No more, no less.'

'Very well, driver, if you say so,' Inspector Branston fumbled. As he turned on his heel in a vain attempt to make a dignified exit in the face of this one-sided battle of words, his dignity deserted him as he tripped over a stray lump of coal. Jock just had time to steady him before the said Inspector took a swallow dive through the still open cab doors.

'I'd climb down if I was you, old son,' Jock said with a half smile and more than a little sarcasm in his voice.

'Yes driver, I will, I will. Well done, well done.'

The last we saw of the mollified Inspector Branston was him hop-scotching across the lines from the sidings in his railway-issue squeaky boots to make his report.

Jock was mumbling incoherently to himself as he polished his shiny topped cap, his face as black as a nun's knickers.

'Bloody morons. They couldn't run a brothel in Cairo. They'd get the bloody camels mixed up with the bloody customers!'

The second trip was a repeat of the first. We just made it with not a breath of steam to spare.

But the third and last trip could present problems, this we knew, the reason being that by now the fire was six hours older, nowhere near as bright and clear as when we had started out. The distinct possibility that she would drop a few pounds in steam pressure at the vital moment was a very real one.

'I'll tell you what we'll do, Jack,' Jock mused as we stood waiting for the signal. 'Instead of notching her up on the gear to give us that bit in reserve, we'll give her the bloody lot from the start. You're going to have a hell of a job to keep any fire in her, but it's the only chance we've got. . .'

Off flew the peg, and off flew 8033. Initially there wasn't much difference. The wheels weren't spinning enough nor were the powerful cylinders pumping enough steam through the blastpipe at this low speed. But no sooner had she picked up her skirts and started waltzing along the mile-long straight leading to the bank when the chimney end reminded me of a Lewis machine-gun in full cry. She was spitting out noise and fire in a flat crescendo.

Over the 'Jack points' we flew. I was firing through the half-open firebox like a demon, but it was a hopeless battle. For every shovel-ful of coal I threw in, Jock blasted two out.

The pressure dropped off the 225 mark back to 200. She noticeably slowed. I shut off the water injector, gave her a quick dozen round the box, slammed the doors shut then shrugged my shoulders in Jock's direction. I could do no more.

The pressure needle crept back up to 210 lbs. Up to 215, then 220. The water level was bobbing dangerously low in the gauge glasses. I reached up to switch on the injector, but Jock yelled 'NO! Leave it. I'd sooner blow a bloody lead plug than let those buggers win!'

'Whoosh' popped the safety valves. 8033 responded by attempting to slip her wheels.

'Don't you bloody well dare,' Jock admonished, shaking a clenched fist at the steel boiler. 'You give one bloody slip and I'll relegate you so low you'll be lucky to end up on shunting duties.'

This was the ultimate insult to any mainline steam engine. That meant the knacker's yard. 8033 wasn't having any of that. Making a last supreme effort she hauled her reluctant train clear of the 'Jack points' and away from any further danger.

'My God, Jack, we've cracked it,' Jock cheered as we blasted through Mansfield Station causing the throng of passengers awaiting the next train to turn tail and beat a hasty retreat in the face of this spitting, snorting monster.

Half an hour later it was all over. As we were signing off Jock placed a friendly arm around my shoulder.

'Come on, Jack, I'm treating you to a couple of pints in Sam's Cabin across the road. I reckon you've earned it.'

The last remark regarding this extraordinary day's work was spoken by Jock in his usual inimitable manner. The time-keeper had popped his head through the window, telephone in hand.

'Control says to tell you "Well done, driver".'

'Yes,' Jock flung back over his shoulder, '. . . tell 'em to get stuffed!'

9
LAUGHS WITH CHARLIE

By early 1944 my friends and I had been employed on the railway for approximately three years. The powers that be had decided that we were old enough and had sufficient experience to be promoted to the exalted position of registered fireman. We were each in turn given a proficiency test by one of the bowler-hatted brigade and duly promoted.

The most important aspect of this earth-shattering decision as far as we were concerned was the extra five shillings a week this would put in our wage packets. A further advantage was that in the future we would be employed solely as firemen, our cleaning days were now a thing of the past.

At this point in the war years we could all clearly see from the extra and, at times, unusual traffic we were called upon to operate that events were beginning to accelerate rapidly. On several occasions we were detailed to take a pair of engines coupled together down to Nottingham where we would be shunted on to a lonely siding away from the public eye, then hooked up to an eleven or twelve-coach train that was completely blacked out with all doors locked and armed soldiers patrolling all sides of the train.

Once we got the 'right away' we would go blasting up the Mansfield bank non-stop to our destination, which was usually Worksop on the LNER line, where we then had running rights. Having arrived there we would uncouple our own LMS engines to make way for the North Eastern men to back their engines on to the train and proceed on the second leg of the journey to God knows where. We never asked, for we knew before-

hand that we would not be given an answer. No doubt they were destined for one of the numerous prisoner-of-war camps that were centred in and around the Midlands.

During the transfer of trains from one railway to another, it was always a ritual that each company stuck to its own motive power. Although all steam engines were fundamentally alike, they were entirely different in looks, design and operation, so it was considered prudent as far as was possible for the crews to stick to the engines they had been brought up with and trained on.

Interspersed with these particular types of trains, we would often be called upon to sign on, again at dead of night - for these trains were always moved during the night hours for reasons of secrecy and safety - to man ammunition or troop trains with just the occasional tank transporter thrown in for good measure. We were usually given two very powerful engines for these jobs, either 'Crab' 2-6-0s or Stanier 'Black Fives'. Many's the time we have travelled light-engine down to Whitwell or Worksop and hooked up to sheeted and camouflaged low-loaders. We knew full well that by giving us such tremendous engines to double-head a train it was likely to prove a very heavy load. And sure enough, when we saw the specially reinforced trucks, albeit camouflaged, there was no mistaking the burden. Army tanks. Twenty to a train, and my God they were heavy! It was fortunate that the engines were designed specifically for this purpose, with a fully-fitted brake throughout. There would have been no stopping this weight with our more conventional loose-coupled wagons, relying entirely on the engine and guard's brake to control them.

As a rule we would work these trains down to Nottingham where we would be turned on to a slip line that ran adjacent to Nottingham Loco. Two sets of men would be waiting to relieve us, who in turn would then drive the train forward through Wellingborough to London where a set of Kentish Town men would finish the long journey to one of the Channel ports.

But, alas, my freedom was to come to an end. In retrospect this is what my previous three years had been. I was to be booked into one of the passenger links with a regular driver as my constant companion for twelve months. It was always the luck of the draw as to whom you would be teamed up with, for, as in all walks of life, men come in all shapes and sizes and attitude, and drivers were no exception to the rule. You considered yourself either lucky or unlucky, depending on

Working nightly wartime traffic, we often had a 'Crab' 2-6-0 and a 'Black Five' double-headed. Here one of each, 'Crab' No 42839 and Stanier '5MT' No 4467, are seen at Nottingham Midland on 12 March 1955. *Derek Murdoch*

the man with whom you were drawn. But they all invariably had one thing in common - they were men of the old school who had been brought up and trained in the old LMS traditions of obedience and discipline. They were all past retiring age and had been asked to continue working for the duration of the war. Their special skills were in very short supply and the pension, being what it was in 1939, amounted to practically nothing. They were only too pleased to be still drawing regular top-line wages.

There were approximately twenty of these drivers working the passenger links, and one could not help but admire them. Although they were, to a man, in the 65 to 70-plus age group, they were physically and mentally capable of putting in a hard week's work at the side of much younger men. This was pretty remarkable when you consider that this entailed signing on for six days a week at three and four o'clock in the morning, for these were the hours of all-day shifts on passenger trains.

The link consisted of five early morning and five afternoon shifts that signed on between midday and two o'clock, making ten different weeks' work in total.

The one to which I was assigned was considered to be the junior of the two links, on which the younger hands were gradually acclimatised to the complexities of passenger work before progressing into the senior link where there were more main-line runs. The stations we were to run between were on the Worksop, Mansfield, Nottingham and Newark lines, added to which were two pull-and-push duties that connected Sutton Town with Sutton Junction, thus making up our ten-week cycle.

The locals knew this pull-and-push service as the 'Penny Emma'. The principle on which it operated was that after running the train engine-first into the station, instead of unhooking and running round the coaches, the driver would walk back to the end coach and position himself in a special compartment before a dual set of controls consisting of regulator and brake. In theory, the fireman was supposed to busy himself with his own duties and utilise the reversing lever under

the driver's instructions via a bell code that was connected between the coaches and the engine. In practice, the only time we used to work according to the Rule Book was if an Inspector was riding with us, but this happened so rarely that the fireman used to work all the controls on the footplate while the driver just kept a weather eye open.

I was indeed fortunate in the allocation of my driver, for I was to be booked with Charlie Jones with whom I enjoyed ten very happy months. He was one of those all too rare characters who are extrovert with an inbuilt sense of fun. You never had a dull moment with Charlie - you were either laughing or arguing, there was no happy medium. I certainly had my share of good-natured arguments with him over politics. He was a dyed-in-the-wool Tory and I was an avowed Socialist. We would become so engrossed in our differences of opinion, often when we were standing in a station, that several of our 'customers', as Charlie used to call them long before the modern BR practice of doing so, would stand there outside the cab listening to us. More than once they were so carried away that they joined in on one side or the other. Indeed, once or twice the arguments became so heated and intense, with a dozen or more people joining in, that the guard, after blowing his whistle and waving his flag, had to come running down the platform to separate us all to get the train under way!

The main trouble was that when he got excited Charlie used to stutter, so badly that it could take him several minutes to utter even a few words. He would always conclude his opinions with the old saying 'F-f-follow the money and you wont g-g-go far wrong'.

My answer to this was always succinct, to the point and certainly unprintable. Anyone listening to us would never have believed that we were really the very best of friends.

Charlie was a strange paradox in some ways: on the one hand he could be as mean as Scrooge, yet on the other he could be generous to a fault. The older drivers who had known him all his life always said of him that, the way he lived, he must own a row of houses.

I was courting strongly by this time and trying to save a little money every week. My wages, being only £3 5s, made this somewhat difficult, so I used to allow myself only five cigarettes a day, but you could guarantee that Charlie would 'borrow', as he called it, at least three of them every shift. Not once did he ever offer to pay me back, and although he smoked like a Class '8' chimney, I never saw him buy a cigarette in his life. All he would say to me when he pinched mine was 'D-D-Don't worry, J-J-Jack. I'll pay you b-b-back at l-l-least d-d-double when the t-t-time c-c-comes.'

I hadn't got a clue what he was talking about. Knowing full well that he never bought any cigarettes, I couldn't for the life of me see how the hell he was ever going to pay me back!

But knowing Charlie as I did, I thought 'Patience, Jack, all will be revealed.' And sure enough, the following week, on days, it was.

There were four weeks out of our ten-week link when we would run into Nottingham and have to wait for around twenty minutes for connections before being due out again. As was usually the case, whenever you ran into any main-line station, all the lads, dads and grandads would come rushing over to look at the engine, but as the majority of our engines were fitted with spring-loaded doors, it was almost impossible for the punters to see over and into the cab. Quite naturally they wanted to be allowed on to the footplate proper which, strictly speaking, was dead against the rules. Nonetheless, Charlie, having got this off to a fine art by this time after years of practice, had decided that all the rules in his book were designed to be bent, if not broken. So his initial response for requests to be allowed on to the footplate would be to look up and down the platform to make certain none of the bowler-hatted brigade were in the vicinity. Then, looking round the customers, he would carefully choose the first victims who would always be men who had a small boy or girl in their charge. The most important ingredient of the plot was that the victims had to be smoking.

I had been thoroughly primed by this time so knew beforehand the role I had to play. The plot never varied. It would unfold itself in the following manner, and rarely failed. I would be lounging casually on the fireman's seat that overlooked the platform whilst Charlie was on the seat opposite, and the number of customers could vary at any given time from around ten to upwards of thirty or more. I would be asked through my open window, usually by a man carrying a child, 'Is it possible to bring the child on to the footplate to have a look round?'

There would be a sharp intake of breath from me with a slow shaking of the head. I would then refuse, reluctantly, quoting the relevant rule, but if by chance the parent happened to be smoking, and most men appeared to be in those days, I would give the thumbs-up signal to Charlie behind my back.

This would be the sign for him to saunter across and enquire what the problem was. I would explain the predicament and after a further glance along the platform to make certain the coast was clear, his next remark would be directed at the customer concerned.

'C-C-Certainly you can bring the child ab-b-board.'

He would snap open the spring doors, usher them both on to the footplate, then slam the doors shut behind them. This made the customer feel very privileged indeed, which was just the reaction we were looking for.

'J-J-Jack, open the firebox d-d-doors and show the child the f-f-fire.'

Charlie would then launch into his well-rehearsed patter.

'I w-w-wonder, sir, could you spare a c-c-cigarette? J-J-Jack and myself are running to such a tight sched. . .sched. . .timetable, you see, that we haven't had the opportunity to leave our engine to b-b-buy any, and we've completely run out.'

It was always a sure-fire winner. Already feeling obligated to us, the customers were prepared to bend over backwards to do us a favour in return. Invariably the answer was the same.

'Certainly, driver, take two or three for yourself and the same for your fireman.'

Or, if it was our lucky day, 'Keep the whole

packet - I can easily get another.'

After we had shown this customer off, and had obliged five or six more smoking victims, by the end of a twenty-minute session we could have acquired around thirty or forty assorted cigarettes and cigars. Also, with Charlie having a pipe handy, which, incidently he never smoked, we had enough tobacco for a few roll-ups. After dividing them equally between us, we had sufficient to last us for quite a few days and, like the squirrel will hoard its nuts for a rainy day, so we used to save our spoils for when we were on the wrong shift and our source of supply was cut off. Apart from holidays, during the whole of the ten months I was booked with Charlie I never once bought any cigarettes!

On one of our early morning shifts we used to work a busy commuter train from Whitwell down to Nottingham. After shunting the empty coaches into the carriage sidings, we would drive our engine into Nottingham Loco, fill her up with water, then position her under the hopper to top up with coal. After turning her off into one of the three roundhouses, we were finished for the day. She would be picked up by a set of men in the afternoon to work the Erewash Valley munitions train back to Mansfield.

We were due to travel passenger to our home depot, but having an hour to spare it was our habit to call on Charlie's brother, Bill, if he was on the right shift, because he was also a driver but stationed at Nottingham. The idea behind our visit was twofold. First, to obtain a free mug of tea, for Charlie didn't believe in paying for anything. Charlie and his brother were like two peas in a pod, not only in looks but also in temperament. They were as mean as the proverbial man with short arms and deep pockets. Where they did differ was in charm. Charlie could wheedle money out of you and you'd honestly believe he was doing you a favour. This was the second and most important reason for the visit. Charlie would succeed in badgering Bill into lending him half-a-crown and, in return, Bill would insist on an IOU.

As soon as we were clear of the house Charlie would laughingly say 'He's got enough of my IOUs to decorate his toilet. Come on, Jack, we've got the price of two pints and a packet of Woodbines here. Let's go and drink our Bill's health.'

Apart from being quite a character, Charlie was also a very good engineman. During the period I was booked with him I completed my apprenticeship to my satisfaction and now considered myself a fully fledged fireman capable of taking on any task that was given to me and being competent enough to give a good account of myself.

The work that drivers and firemen were called upon to do was often complex and demanding. We were expected to be equally proficient with any engine on any train travelling in any direction at all hours of the day or night. It was not enough just to have the ability to work one train, which was often quite a job in itself - you had to multiply this

In the roundhouse at Nottingham Loco, ex-LMS Class '5MT' 4-6-0 No 45154 *Lanarkshire Yeomanry* in the centre. September 1957. *Derek Murdoch*

many times over to fully appreciate the complexities of the career we had chosen. It was a remark made by Charlie one day, in railway jargon, that convinced me that I had finally made it.

'Once a fireman can fire by the chimney end, he's through with training.'

The true significance of this statement didn't really strike me until I realised that this was precisely the way I had been handling different engines for the last three months!

To attempt to describe what this means in a few words, having taken me three years to learn it, is well nigh impossible. To 'fire by the chimney end' was a combination of many things, including the types of engine you were handling; some made smoke more readily than others, and some needed a thicker body of fire in order to steam efficiently. Coal trains called for a constant steady supply of steam, while a Class 'A' fitted-brake freight required similar conditions to a passenger train, steam in short, sharp bursts.

The kind of gradients you were running over were also important. Often you had to plan ahead and have the fire and steam pressure spot on to meet an approaching uphill stretch. The quality of the coal with which you were firing also made a difference. Slack or small coal produced smoke more readily than lumps. Your driver was an added complication. Some would be able to keep time in addition to working the engine economically, whilst others would go flat out and to hell with the poor old fireman.

The theory behind these innumerable problems agreed, for once, with the practical side. Steam, being an invisible gas until it comes into contact with the air, would not manifest itself until it had been blasted clear of the chimney end by approximately 12 inches, but smoke was visible at all times. The seven or eight inches above the rim of the chimney was the guideline on which was based all the calculations for the conclusion you should arrive at by a mere glance through the cab window, having taken into account all the possible permutations.

Today, an engineer requiring the solution to a problem has an amazing range of modern technology, back-up systems and computer wizardry to help him find the answer. In those days of steam, all the fireman had to help him get it right was three or four years of solid, practical railway experience, a feeling for what he was doing and a love for his chosen profession. You cannot lift experience from the pages of a book. You have to live it and, in the hard grinding process, learn the finer points of your craft. And so it was with firemen.

But once this knowledge was locked in your brain you could tell with one glance, instinctively, not only if your fire needed replenishing, but by how much and where.

One further problem, as if any more were needed, was that in sharp frosty weather steam would show the instant it met cold air, whereas hot weather produced the opposite effect. In fact, with perfect combustion, the engine could be blasting away and all that would be visible was a very fine emission, light grey in colour. This really gives the lie to the opinions of the uninitiated who persist in their beliefs that a steam engine is a dirty machine that produces copious amounts of thick black smoke. An experienced fireman could so manage his fire that even today's environmentalists would be hard put to complain.

10

THE GOOD OLD DAYS

My ten happy months with Charlie passed all too quickly; all good things come to an end and my time spent with him was no exception.

I was next booked with another driver of the old school, but one who was totally devoid of Charlie's wit and sense of fun. His name was Tommy West and, fortunately, we were only together for a period of three months. I say fortunately because some of his habits were, to say the least, unnerving. He was evidently a highly religious man, but at the time I had no knowledge of this. If I had known I would not have been so taken by surprise with some of his idiosyncrasies.

For example, after having been given the 'right away' at Mansfield on receiving the green flag and whistle from the guard, off we would trot on our day's travel. All would be well for the first two or three stations, then, on a sudden impulse, he'd jump off his driver's seat, leaving all the controls to their own devices as we bowled merrily along. He'd push me to one side if I happened to be firing and would start walking round the footplate in tight little circles singing at the top of his voice 'Now thank we all our God', or one of his other favourite hymns from his quite remarkable repertoire. How on earth he maintained his main-line status heaven knows.

I collapsed on to my seat looking at him in fear and amazement - we were belting along at 60 miles per hour at the time with the train being left to drive itself! Suddenly, again for no apparent reason, he'd stop his singing, sit back in his seat and carry on driving as though all this was perfectly normal.

Perhaps to him it was, but it scared the living daylights out of me. This pantomime was to be repeated at frequent intervals during the whole of the three months I was booked with him.

He also had a nasty habit of doing a disappearing act. I'd turn around at times to make some remark and there he was - or rather wasn't. He'd gone. I thought 'My God, he's fallen off!' and go rushing over to find him calmly walking along the catwalk of the engine, hanging on for dear life with one hand and carrying his oilcan in the other, still singing hymns loud enough to be heard above the roar of the engine.

Shortly after, I left him to take a further step forward in my career on the footplate. I was to be promoted into the senior passenger link. Within a month Tom was taken off main line to finish his time on local shunt duties. I'm pretty certain that if some of the passengers had realised who they were riding behind, depending upon their denomination, they would have held communion, visited the synagogue more regularly or made a last trip to Mecca to make sure of a booking in the hereafter.

The driver I was to be booked with in the senior link was named Alf Botham, another one of the old-timers who had spent about fifty years on the footplate, progressing through the LMS and its predecessors.

Alf was 68, but despite the difference in our ages we got on remarkably well, which, as I have stressed previously, was a great advantage, particularly in this link, for on most of the runs it was hard work with very little respite. We had the Sheffield job that I have described earlier, the 5.56 Erewash to Nottingham, the 5.30 Whitwell that made up the busy 7.20 commuter train to Nottingham, plus the run that was universally disliked, without exception, by everyone in the link, the 1.15 Nottingham.

A brief description will suffice to show why this dislike was unanimous. Having signed on at 12.40 in the afternoon with the engine being prepared for us, we picked up the coaches from the sidings, then down to the station ready for departure at 1.15 all stations to Nottingham. After filling the water tanks we had twenty minutes before being due away at 2.30 for Newark. At 3.15 we pulled into our destination with half an hour to run round the train, fill the tanks, clean the fire, and in the five minutes remaining

Ex-London, Tilbury & Southend Railway '79' Class 4-4-2T No 41940, with LMS on the tanks but carrying its new BR number, at Nottingham. We called them 'crooners', these Mansfield-based locos on which I sweated for so many years. They were universally disliked by footplate crews throughout the Midland Division. *J. F. Henton*

just have time for a sandwich and a drink of warm tea from a bottle, for on this type of run there wasn't sufficient time for such luxuries as a freshly made billy-can of tea. The next best thing was a bottle kept warm on the 'dish-plate'. You can well imagine how it tasted after stewing for eight hours.

On leaving Newark at 3.45, we knew that there was a three-hour slog facing us calling at all stations back to Nottingham, where we filled the tanks and became the 4.50 to Mansfield; here we filled up once more, as these engines only held 1,500 gallons of water. Then we took the 6.15 all stations to Worksop - same procedure as at Newark, fill up, clean out the fire and away again back to Mansfield at 7.20, arriving at 8.10. Finally we shunted the coaches and pulled into the Loco dead on eight hours after signing on.

We worked this same train for six days a week without one minute's overtime. For this I would receive the magnificent remuneration of £4 10s a week, a paltry sum when you consider that in each eight hour shift we travelled 120 miles, stopped at 48 stations,

filled the tanks six times, cleaned the fire twice, burned five tons of coal, and more often than not took home our sandwiches as there had been no time to enjoy them. Particularly during the summer months I used to carry a spare quart bottle of water which, during the day's work, I'd fill at least four times. I'm not sure how, but I'll guarantee that for every pint drunk I'd sweat two. I was often wet through during the whole shift - no wonder my weight never topped eight stone.

Don't tell me about the good old days - there weren't any!

It was during the time I was booked with Alf that my girfriend, Maisie, and I decided to get married. Or to be more accurate, we had it decided for us by my future father-in-law. We awoke on the day in question to discover ourselves in the middle of a real pea-souper of a fog. Consequently, instead of having the knot tied for us at eleven in the morning, we had to rearrange the time with the vicar, and seeing as no taxis would turn out, walk the five miles to the church to be married at three in the afternoon. Still, all's

Annesley Station, one of the 48 stations at which we stopped on the dreaded 1.15 Nottingham turn. This view is dated 1953 - the station closed to passenger, parcels and freight traffic shortly after. *Nottingham Evening Post*

well that ends well, for we are still together after 47 years - bit of a record I would imagine with today's generation!

The following months that I spent with Alf Botham were, to say the least, accident-prone. Pure coincidence, of course, but the Gods above weren't smiling on me at the time. We were busy working the 1.15 to Nottingham one day in January (this was the train, you will remember, where having run into Worksop at 7.15, I had a mere twenty minutes in which to clean the fire sufficiently to get us back up the bank to Mansfield). I was trying to force the 'straight dart', the ten-foot steel rod pointed at the end like an arrow, along the fire bars to loosen the clinker that had formed during the day's work, thus allowing the air to circulate through the fire, when, having managed to slide it along for about six feet, I was attempting to both lift and twist at the same time. I can only imagine that I misjudged the pivot point. Instead of the dart lifting as I thrust downwards I felt a sudden agonising pain in my back - it was so intense I must have cried out.

Alf came rushing back on to the footplate to see what was wrong and discovered me stretched out all my length on the floorboards. It was utterly impossible for me to move in any direction - any movement brought instant agony. After about fifteen minutes, with the assistance of one of the porters, they managed to lift me off the floor and up into my seat where they secured me with a length of rope. I hardly dared move a muscle all the way home to Mansfield. To Alf's great credit, he not only drove the engine, but managed to do the firing and work the injectors.

Back at the Loco they lifted me off the engine, put me on my bike and gave me a push. Somehow I made it back home, even though it took me an hour and a half. No sooner had I arrived home when out came the old favourite, the horse liniment. Forty years on I still suffer from that same injury and over the years I must have used enough rubbing oils to keep half a dozen massage parlours happy. Even so, as was usual in those days, I was back at work the following day, but the shift seemed to last twenty-four hours. As the weeks passed, exercise and movement eased things a little and the pain wore off.

I had just about mastered this problem when, quite out of the blue, up popped another. We were on the 5.30 am Whitwell at the time and, thankfully, were nearing the end of the shift. On this particular day the engine had been coaled with very large lumps that I had to keep breaking up into a more manageable size. The coal worked its way forward due to the movement and sway of the engine, and I was attempting to break up one of the particularly large pieces with the pointed end of the pick when the point sliced straight through a soft seam in the coal as though it were made of butter and carried on through my boot and foot, pinning me to the floorboards beneath. I believe even an old-timer like Alf heard a few words on this occasion that were new to him. I was well aware that the most painful part was yet still to come - I had to pull the damn thing out! The mere thought of it brought me out in a cold sweat, but out it had to come.

There was only one way - a quick pull and

A fireman using a pick to break up large lumps of coal. It was a pick such as this that pinned me to the floorboards when I mis-aimed. The scene is Rugby, in July 1938. G. A. Barlow, *Mac Johnstone collection*

it was all over. It was not so bad as I had imagined, and having taken off my boot and sock I realised just how fortunate I had been. The pick had driven itself clean between two toes, and even though they were cut and bleeding, it could have been much worse. I washed my foot in the bucket of water, wrapped my handkerchief around it and carried on. Although I was hopping around like a kangaroo for the next few days, I appreciated just how lucky I had been.

One of the highlights of our week, and God knows there weren't many, was pay day. Alf and myself, providing we were on the right shift, would meet up at Mansfield Station where all the railwaymen would congregate to receive our weekly 'fortune'. After joining the queue we were expected to shout out our number - mine was 153. A small tin with our number stamped on to the lid would then be passed out to us, we would empty the contents, then hand back the tin ready for use the following week. The railway company had not as yet attained the exalted luxury of issuing pay packets. Oh boy, it was great! For a few hours, until the elation wore off, we were actually rich.

The first stop for Alf and myself would be the Midland Hotel across the road. Alf never failed to bring his dog, Sally, with him. This was a treat for her too. There would be two pints of bitter for Alf and me and a half pint for Sally. She was very choosy - she didn't like bitter, but you should have seen her knock the mild back. She'd always polish off her half pint before we were half way through our pints. We usually stayed for about an hour, or until Sally keeled over, whichever came sooner, then we'd go our respective ways, me on my bike and Alf carrying Sally. I could never really work out who usually ended up the more inebriated, Alf on his two legs or Sally on her four!

Above right **Mansfield Station, where we used to receive our weekly fortune. A 1990 view.** *Author*

Right **The Midland Hotel, my first stop after receiving said weekly fortune, to meet Alf and his dog, Sally.** *Author*

On one of our mid-morning Nottingham runs they tacked on an additional trip at twelve noon to Burton Joyce and Lowdham for the midday commuters, thus enabling them to go home for their lunch. After 'running round' the coaches, we were then turned into the sidings to await the return journey at 1.15. This was a pleasant little diversion in more ways than one. If I had a young-hand driver with me, as was often the case due to illness or holidays, then for him there was the added attraction of the, by now, numerous young lady guards in charge of this train. Well, you can imagine the rest - you don't need me to tell you. But I will anyway.

I particularly remember one day as we were backing into the sidings. Fred, a passed fireman who was very partial to Irene, the lady guard, left me in sole charge as he jumped down from the footplate and hopped up into the guard's van to 'have his lunch and a mug of tea with Irene', as he tactfully put it. I suspected he was having more than just a tasty snack with her.

As soon as he'd climbed aboard the coach, down came the blinds, and even after the signals came off for us to draw into the platform, there was still no sign of Fred. At the very last minute when we were due to depart, down the platform he chased, looking red faced and decidedly flustered. At the same moment Irene put in an appearance, also looking somewhat dishevelled and in such a state that she couldn't make up her mind whether to wave the green flag or the red one.

On reflection I thought it just as well that Fred was only booked with me for a week, or he'd have to have had a few weeks in a rest home to recuperate. Our Irene had earned quite a reputation with the lads - I honestly believe she put more drivers and firemen on the sick list than Adolf Hitler ever did.

I was still booked with Alf when the war ended in 1945. Within a couple of months of the end of hostilities, due to the fact that there was a great influx of men returning from the armed forces, the twenty drivers who had been retained over their time were compulsorily retired. By this time most of them were knocking on 70, and to attempt to illustrate their dedication to the role of being top-link passenger drivers and their status, respected by all the people with whom they came into contact, is well nigh impossible. Suffice it to say that within eighteen months of their retirement, nineteen of the twenty drivers had died from one cause or another, but all who knew them had their own theory about this phenomenon. Their reason for living had been taken away from them, for these were no ordinary men. They were a special breed, the like of which we shall never see again.

The railway was their life. They lived, breathed and slept it. To a man they had

A recent view of Lowdham Station, looking east, the scene of Irene's and Fred's not so innocent little diversions. *Author*

Carlton & Netherfield Station was another call on the Lowdham run. Here it is pictured on the occasion of winning the 'Best Kept Station Award' in 1964. *Nottingham Evening Post*

been on the footplate for the best part of fifty years, and, I believe, in retrospect, during the greatest years of railway history.

They had assimilated and accepted the deprivations and hardships that were the common lot of all footplate staff, and were so on top of their job that they actually relished it. The harder and more difficult the tasks they were set, the harder they would strive to overcome them. You either beat them or went under - there were no half measures in those days and such was the character of these unique men that they always, without exception, won through. I admired them tremendously. Even at my early age I could sense that they were men of exceptional skills and ability.

I remarked earlier that they had all died but one. And you don't need two guesses as to who the survivor was. Yes, you're right, Charlie Jones. To the best of my knowledge he was still alive and kicking in the mid-

1980s, when he must have been well over 90.

After Alf's retirement I was paired with one of the much younger drivers who had been promoted, much against their will, from the goods link where life had been comparatively easy, into the passenger links where you had to earn every penny you received. His name was Billy Brunt.

During the summer of 1946 my wife was taken into hospital as a precaution against what was envisaged as being a difficult time over the birth of our first child. The hospital at Basford in Nottingham where Maisie was taken was 14 miles from our home in Skegby, so the only drawback to this enforced stay was getting down to see her after finishing work. As the bus service was extremely haphazard, it usually turned out to be a three or four-hour stint to visit her. We did have one piece of luck on our side in that the hospital was situated only 200 yards away from our main line into Nottingham over which I was working most days. It was also very fortunate for us that the hospital was only half a mile away from Basford Station, one of our stops.

As is often the case with the first-born,

David, as we later named him, refused to appear on the given date. He's never altered - he's still always late for appointments. It seemed to me at the time that Maisie was becoming a permanent resident at the hospital, and as it was proving very difficult for me to visit her as often as I would have liked, we arranged between us a type of code. We were able to contrive this as Maisie had been given a bed next to the window that overlooked our line and, as she knew the timings of the trains through Basford Station on which I would be firing, she had a fairly accurate idea of when to listen out for me.

The arrangement we made was that on leaving the station I would give her three sharp blasts on the engine whistle. This would allow her just one minute to hop out of her bed and stand at the window so that we could wave to one another. The reason behind this subterfuge was that if Maisie was standing against the window in what was known as the 'How Much Bloody Longer?' ward, she quite obviously wasn't in the 'Mission Accomplished' ward.

The plan worked perfectly for the first two or three days, but the old adage 'The best laid plans of mice and men. . .' certainly applied in our case. All the passenger crews centred at my home Loco quickly cottoned on to our code and, believing they were helping us, all decided to get in on the act. Consequently, every train that pulled out of Basford Station - and they were many and varied - used to whistle Mais' up to such an extent that she was in and out of bed like a fiddler's elbow.

Even some of the passengers decided to join in the game and could be seen leaning out of the carriage windows waving their arms and handkerchiefs. When we all arrived back at the Loco at about twelve o'clock after our respective runs, it was our collective habit to congregate in the messroom for about ten minutes before signing off to compare notes. I would be regaled at least a dozen times by different firemen with same old story.

'She hasn't had it yet, Jack. She stood at the window and waved to us.'

It became so noisy around the hospital with engine whistles going off at all hours of the day and night that the Matron made an official complaint as patients couldn't get to sleep. If they did, we woke them all up again! An order appeared on the noticeboard forbidding the use of engine whistles in the vicinity of the hospital except in the case of an emergency. Personally, I totally ignored this order - for me this was an emergency!

Even so, Maisie managed to dupe me. On the fifteenth morning of her incarceration I whistled her up as usual and there she was, standing at the window in her nightie waving to me as usual. I couldn't help but think 'My God, how much longer?' As I was due to visit her that night I didn't feel too bad about it, at least we would be able to sit and talk.

I turned up at my regular time, seven o'clock, made my way up to the 'How Much Bloody Longer Ward?' and made a bee-line for Maisie's bed, as near as dammit giving my flowers to the wrong woman as I put my arms around her. I extricated myself from her clutches just in time to stop her screaming the place down. Hurriedly apologising, I backed off. I didn't fancy her anyway - she wasn't half as pretty as my Mais'.

As luck would have it the Ward Sister had followed me in and must have witnessed this wicked assault within her hallowed halls. She gave me a withering look over the top of her pince-nez then started to lay into me as though I was son of Jack The Ripper!

'Honest, Sister,' I mumbled, 'I've been coming to this same bed to visit my wife for the last fifteen days - I thought she'd become a permanent fixture. She waved as usual this morning, so naturally I expected her to be in her usual bed.'

On hearing these words her face went as stiff as her apron.

'So! You're the nuisance that's been keeping my patients awake!'

I had to think fast on my feet for this one - she was like a female Blaster Bowen.

'No, Sister, not me. It's my wife's brother, it's him. He works on the railway, you see. It's him - not me.'

I then told her I was attending medical school studying for a degree that specialises in Obstetrics. A remarkable change came over her. It was like salt changing into sugar, or night becoming day. She personally escorted me into the 'Mission Accomplished Ward', instructing the duty nurse to make sure that I enjoyed every comfort during my stay. When she left she was smiling sweetly, no doubt thinking that one day I might be her future boss.

The outcome of all this subterfuge was that Maisie had given birth to David at twelve noon. Although in labour at the time, she had somehow managed to make her way to the window to give me the 'all clear' signal to prevent causing me any unnecessary worry. Even then her thoughts were first and foremost for me, which is still her very unselfish attitude to this day.

Meanwhile, back on the job, I have often heard stories of how women can become so engrossed in having a good gossip that they can become totally oblivious to the world around them. We were to experience this phenomenon at first hand one cold December day in 1946.

Billy Brunt and I had been detailed to work a special passenger train non-stop from

Maisie and David, 1946, now safely home from the clutches of the Sister. *Author*

Mansfield to Nottingham. After passing through Kirkby and Annesley Tunnel we started to accelerate rapidly down the bank towards Hucknall, six miles distant. On a clear day Hucknall came into immediate view for the line is as straight as an arrow.

It was a sharp crisp morning with about nine inches of snow laying on the surrounding countryside. The only contrast to this white blanket was the twin sets of black lines stretching away into the distance. As we were booked non-stop we were now beginning to rattle along at 60 or 70 miles per hour with all signals showing clear. We were about four miles from Hucknall, where the speed would need to be checked slightly as the platform stood on a curve, when I looked down the track. I could just make out two faint dots in the middle of the line silhouetted against the white background. As there was a pedestrian crossing at this point we at first took little notice, but as we rapidly lessened the distance, we identified the dots as two people, and they were static. By now, being only two miles from them, Bill had started to apply the brakes whilst I gave them several sharp blasts on the whistle.

Still no sign of movement from them.

We could now make them out as being two women standing with their backs to us. Our engine, not having steam on, was blowing off through both safety valves and making one hell of a row.

Again I whistled them up, and Bill had the brake slammed hard across to try and stop the train if the necessity arose. Still a mile from them, we naturally anticipated that when they eventually did hear us, or felt the rumble of the track beneath their feet, they'd move.

We drew nearer and nearer still, Bill desperately trying to stop the train. I left the whistle wide open. And that, with both safety valves blowing off at full cock, produced such an absolutely deafening sound that it would have awoken the dead.

But not these two. They remained rooted to the spot, oblivious to the hundreds of tons of steel thundering down towards them.

This may sound so impossible, so unbelievable, that it beggars the truth, but take my word for it, it's an absolute fact. We finally managed to bring the train to a shuddering halt just twenty yards short of them. If we'd have started to slip they'd have stood no chance whatsoever - they would have become part of the track for all time!

Still they stood there nattering away a hundred to the dozen with their backs to us amidst this deafening crescendo.

I climbed down off the footplate, walked the few steps that separated us, tapped them both on the shoulders, and as they turned, pointed to our engine looming menacingly over the top of them, still making an ear-shattering roar. Their first reaction was one of total fear and disbelief. They turned as white as the snow that surrounded them and screamed at the top of their voices, but the screams were lost, absorbed by the greater, awful noise of the engine.

They turned and bolted for the gate which led off the track and ran for their lives. One of them didn't get very far - she dropped in the snow in a dead faint and we spent the next few minutes trying to revive her. Lucky for her, a policemen who happened to be passing at the time applied his knowledge of first aid and brought her round.

The only possible explanation I can give for their extraordinary behaviour is that they had become so engrossed in their conversation that they had shut the rest of the world out. I still wonder what it was they were talking about that proved so interesting, so absorbing. But there was no doubt in my mind whatsoever, that if we hadn't spotted them in good time, or conversely hadn't been able to stop the train, they would have been very dead indeed!

11
PASSIONATE PERCY

After completing my year with Bill I was booked with another of the unwilling bunch of young drivers who had been promoted out of the cushy freight links on to passenger trains.

I can only describe the six months I spent with Percy Adams as hilarious. It was as well I only enjoyed six months with him before he was promoted - I would never have survived a year. Not at the pace he lived. He wore me out just watching him, and I was twenty years his junior.

He was a great driver to be booked with. He had a marvellous sense of humour and he didn't give a damn for anything or anybody. But there was one facet of his character that drove him, and everyone closely connected with him, to utter distraction. His love of the ladies. He couldn't keep his hands off them, literally. He was totally absorbed and fascinated by them. The sight of a well-turned ankle, or the merest glimpse of a lace-edged petticoat would drive him into a frenzy. It was a driving force within him that could never be stilled nor permanently satisfied. He had certainly been blessed with the right surname, if we are to believe the Bible, and Adam really did start the explosion of mankind. Percy Adams, following him up a few years later, certainly kept the momentum going. He was insatiable.

Once the initial shock of being wrenched away from the easy life that all and sundry had enjoyed in the freight links had worn off, Percy was delighted with his new-found status. Whilst life on goods trains was money for old rope, it was also a very lonely life. But on passengers, Percy was surrounded by ladies!

Ladies, in all shapes and sizes, all ages, all colours. Red-heads, blondes, brunettes, they were all the same to Percy. He loved them all - well, more than his fair share, anyway.

There were none too fat or too thin, too tall or too short, for as Percy would laugh, 'they're all the same size laying down!'

He was incorrigible. No one would have guessed from his antics that he was a happily married man with two charming daughters. Percy personified to absolute perfection what everybody imagined a Don Juan to be. Six feet tall, iron grey hair, and deep brown eyes that must have melted the heart of many a lonely woman. He was slim, smart, and with such a line of patter that the fair sex were like putty in his hands. He really could charm the birds off the trees, but it wasn't the feathered variety of bird that Percy had in mind.

I had a foretaste of what was to come during our first week's work together. We were booked on the 4 pm all stations down to Nottingham, thence to work the 9 pm up the Erewash Valley back to Mansfield. I did all the driving on this week's work, at Percy's request, just until he got the feel of things.

That was his explanation, anyway. In reality it was merely an excuse to allow him complete freedom to roam anywhere his fancy took him. And his fancy took him off the engine and on to the platform where his commanding figure could be seen pointing out what went where and what platform to catch it from. He was extremely courteous and helpful to the ladies, but if you happened to be a man making enquiries you stood no chance. 'Go and ask a porter,' would be his brisk, offhand reply.

This was the pattern that emerged through our first three days' work together, but on the fourth, having found his feet, Percy swung into action. We were standing on platform 5 at 8.30 pm with half an hour to go before receiving the 'right away'. It was a cold November night with the wind gusting unhindered across the open platform. As he leaned out of the engine cab, on the passenger side of course, Percy's beady eyes fastened on to the lovely figure of a lady looking round her as if undecided which way to turn. She was in her late thirties I would guess, more a handsome face than a pretty one, but a nice face for all that. Percy was off our engine like a greyhound out of trap three - this was too good an opportunity to miss. She had neared our engine by this time so I was privy to the conversation and meaningful glances that passed between them.

Percy's voice was solicitous, almost endearing, as he enquired if he could be of any assistance to her. Her query as to our destination was in a throaty whisper. She continued, 'I'm a stranger in these parts, you see, I'm on a visit to see my newly married sister at Pye Bridge.'

'Then look no further, my dear,' Percy assured her. 'Just leave yourself in my hands.'

They stood facing one another on this cold platform and, my God, even with my limited experience of the fairer sex I saw the lightning flash. She transfixed his eyes, her own unflinching. Her colour heightened into a soft blush, her free hand unconsciously smoothing an invisible wrinkle from the side of her pencil-thin skirt.

Percy had drawn himself up to his full height, shoulders pulled right back. For a few brief moments no words passed between them. None were necessary. Both knew what the next move would be. It was inevitable. Her unflinching eyes saw the strong protective man, the one to lean on in a crisis. A man she would yield to.

But in looking into the depths of Percy's eyes, her softer, more emotional female mind also saw a future. Possibly a new beginning, a new start after the initial physical explosion that they both knew was about to take place.

Her slim frame trembled. Maybe it was the cold wind gusting through the station, or it could have been anticipation of the unknown. Percy held out his hands, one to take the suitcase, the other to take her hand which she willingly surrendered.

The first compartment next to our engine was empty, and a young couple approached as if they were about to enter it.

'No!' Percy commanded in an imperious voice. 'This one is reserved.'

He then flung open the door and helped the lady as she stepped sedately inside. He followed, slamming the door behind him. 'Surely not on the platform!' I gasped to myself. 'Even Percy daren't risk that. Not with all the bowler-hat brigade that this main-line station warrants. They could pounce at any moment. . .'

But no, Percy had other plans. Five minutes before take-off he stepped back on to the footplate, a look of sheer wonderment spreading across his face.

'Jack,' he whispered, 'I think I've fallen in love!'

I didn't take too much notice of this earth-shattering announcement. If rumour had it right, Percy fell in love at least once a week. Always it was the love of his life, the end of the rainbow - Fred Astaire and Ginger Rogers, Rhett Butler and Scarlett O'Hara. But Percy's love stories ended as most love stories ended. There was no dancing off into the golden sunset, no lovelorn figures running towards each other, arms outstretched on the lonely cliff-top. No, his love stories ended simply because he always found someone else to fall in love with. But perhaps this latest encounter, this enchanting and wonderful paramour, really would be the love of his life. Only time would tell. It would have to run its course.

Trouble was, its course started running a damn sight sooner than I'd expected. At the first station we ran into there was little likelihood of any bowler-hatted gestapo being around. Percy jumped off the engine on the blind side of the station with the words 'I've put a good fire on, Jack, you've got a full pot of water, see you soon.'

He leapt on to the first step of the passenger compartment then disappeared from view. Even before I got the green flag from the guard the lights had gone out in the boudoir of the lady in question and the blinds pulled firmly down.

The engine presented me with no problems. I was able to work the injectors on the driver's side, and Percy's fire lasted me through to Pye Bridge, the station at which this wondrous lady of the night was due to alight. Sure enough, no sooner had I brought the train to a halt than she stepped sedately on to the platform on one side of the coach, while Percy bundled himself unceremoniously out on the other. He then rushed across the footplate to join her.

She looked radiant and fulfilled.

Percy looked a shattered wreck. He hardly had the strength to stand, let alone lift her suitcase as he escorted her out of the station. The railway system ground to a halt while he gave her a last passionate kiss. She then disappeared into the long shadows of the night as quickly and as mysteriously as she had arrived.

Percy staggered back on to the footplate and slumped wearily into his seat. Burning curiosity got the better of me.

'Well, who is she?'

'I don't know,' Percy muttered.

'Well, what's her name then?

'I don't know.'

'Do you know where she comes from?'

'No.'

'Do you mean to say. . .?' I asked incredulously.

'Yes. You know as much about her as I do. Well, from the outside anyway.'

'But. . .when are you seeing her again? Are you seeing her again?'

He caught his breath. 'I forgot to ask. I was too busy, probably thinking about the train. My God,' he whispered, 'I've heard of "Wham, bang, thank you, ma'm", but this was bloody ridiculous. . .'

We had the seven-mile bank up to Kirkby facing us now, and Percy was definitely in no fit condition to fire, so I suggested that we swap roles. He heaved a sigh of relief: 'You can say that again.'

The rest of the journey was covered in complete silence. Percy was deep in thought, lost in his own little world, no doubt dreaming of the fairer sex.

Needless to say, for weeks afterwards whenever our travels took us through Pye Bridge Percy's eyes would eagerly scan the platform searching for the love of his life. He would even delay the train for a few minutes to give him just that little bit more time. But never a sign of her. It seemed as though she had vanished off the face of the earth.

That is, until one night about two months later as we pulled in with our 10 pm semi-fast to Nottingham which connected up with the 'Midnight Scotsman'.

And there she was, standing underneath one of the flickering station lamps looking directly up into Percy's deep brown eyes, a light smile on her ruby red lips. Percy almost fell off the engine. He was in such a state he didn't know whether to blow the whistle or put the fire out. She beckoned, lifting her eyes suggestively. I've never seen Percy move so fast in his life. Naturally, I was once more left in sole charge to run the LMS Railway.

It was a repeat performance of Pye Bridge when we arrived at Nottingham Station. She went one side, he the other. He was far too besotted to calculate the risks he was taking. The trouble was, we were late in due to signal checks and the 'Scotsman' stood panting, impatient to be off and on its way up to the North. Percy just had time to hurry her through an open carriage as he bundled her suitcase in after her when, with a warning hoot and a great whoosh of steam, the 'Scotsman', headed by a giant Stanier 'Five X', hustled its train out of the station into the night.

'Well?' I asked. 'Surely by now you know more about her.'

'No, there wasn't time.'

'But surely you must know her name?

'Oh, yes,' he whispered, 'I know her name alright. Elizabeth. It's Elizabeth,' he said softly.

But Elizabeth vanished forever out of Percy's life. Oh, he still continued to look for her. He was still looking years afterwards, but their paths never crossed again.

I had my own theory, and that's all it was,

about what happened, and why. Perhaps the first clue was right there on Nottingham Station when they first met. Perhaps it was her voice that gave her away. It was cultured, refined, the voice of a lady with background and breeding. The more I thought about it the more certain I became. Her clothes were elegant and expensive, the luggage possibly Harrods. This was no mill girl from the North. She had the air and the disposition of a lady who could captivate a man by the mere crook of her finger. She lacked nothing in a material sense, but the one thing she needed could not be bought over the counter in a store. The more I reflected on it, the more I formed the opinion, the definite impression, that she was a rich man's plaything. A mistress, a courtesan, call it what you will - I had read somewhere about such women.

Their lives were full of boredom, of dinner parties, of having to say the right thing to the right people. They led lives of inane, decorative, useless chatter. And, sometimes, just the odd time here and there, they kicked over the traces. Their emotions exploded. Their desperation and their boredom drove them to taste the vibrant contrasts of life in the raw, to see how the other half lived and loved.

Percy, in my humble opinion, had merely been the vehicle for the mad passionate affair she craved. Having indulged and sated her wild appetites and whims, she had cast him aside, as he had cast women aside, and returned to her idle, boring useless life.

To her contemporaries she would pretend that nothing out of the ordinary had happened. And I'm sure that, in her own mind, nothing did. The encounter with Percy was fast, furious, passionate and, I've no doubt, by now forgotten.

Prudently I decided to keep my theories to myself. There seemed no point whatsoever in telling him that he had been a rich girl's plaything, a fanciful whim with no substance. And why disillusion him when, for weeks afterwards, in his more private moments he could be heard to whisper 'Elizabeth. . .' as he shook his head slowly in disbelief. 'Why did she never come back to me? Why?'

He must have still been dreaming about Elizabeth one rainy night a couple of months later when catastrophe struck. Our train had been taken over by one of the bowler-hat brigade who was putting a registered fireman through his paces preparatory to him being passed as a driver. This led us to be called in for shed duties helping to get the engines sorted out ready for their respective runs the following morning.

We had a complete line-full to pull out of number one bay to leave room at the bottom for a dead engine that needed its brakes renewing. Having hooked all six engines on to a mighty Class '8', No 8132, we cleared the lot with one hefty pull. The dead engine in question, 3772, a Midland Class '3' freight, was then run out of a slip road that led directly into the relevant bay.

'No need to hook her up Jack,' Percy called, 'I'll just give her a push - you stop her with the hand brake.'

He clanged on to her with his Class '8' and she rolled nice and slowly down to the welded six-inch stops on the end of the bay. I screwed the brakes on to steady her down but they had no effect. She just kept on rolling, and rolling. I hit the brake handle with a pick-axe in an attempt to make them bite, but with the lines and the rails being greasy and wet from the rain outside my efforts were useless. 3772 was sick of the smoke and darkness. She wanted some fresh air and nothing was going to stop her getting it. Trouble was, there was no door at that end, only a solid brick wall, or at least there was until five seconds later when this stubborn cantankerous runaway engine demolished it to make her own door. I'll bet she felt quite proud of her own efforts at knocking down brick walls to provide emergency exits. But she was determined to do it, and do it she did without any help from me.

'Stop her!' Percy screamed at the top of his voice.

'I'm bloody trying to!' I screamed back.

Bump. She tip-toed over the stops with all twelve wheels, and carried on across the cobbled walkway as though glad to be rid of her restraining lines, straight through the brick wall as though it were made of cream cheese.

She then rolled gently across a further twelve yards of rough ground and finally came to rest with her nose leaning delicately against a three-foot-thick stone wall. Behind her, 3772 had left a perfect silhouette where she had crashed through the Loco wall. There wasn't

Top Ex-Midland Class '3F' 0-6-0 No 3637 at Nottingham, of the same class as runaway 3772. . . *G. A. Barlow, Mac Johnstone collection*

Above . . .and Class '8F' No 8132, her downfall and her rescuer, pictured many years later at Nottingham Victoria in the early 1960s. *Author*

a brick out of place. The outline was so precise that even the chimney shape was correct to an inch on either side. In fact, you could have taken a mould and turned out some pretty good replicas!

Percy's white face peered through the hole in the wall. 'What happened?' he asked fearfully.

I couldn't give him a ready answer immediately, I was still trying to extricate myself from the choking brick dust and rubble that had fallen down around my shoulders like confetti at a wedding, even though I'd been cowering on the floorboards hard up against the boiler. I wasn't going to play the hero - I just wanted to keep on living. Well, at least until snap-time.

'What happened?' I shouted at him. 'I'll tell you what bloody happened. You shoved her too bloody hard and the brakes wouldn't bloody well work, that's what bloody well happened!'

I was still trying to shake the soot and cement out of my hair ten minutes later, muttering to myself 'What bloody happened? She's got a will of her own, this bugger.'

By this time the remainder of the night shift had put in an appearance to ascertain the cause of all this crashing and banging. They weren't used to being woken out of their nocturnal slumber by men actually working - it was unheard of. Twenty white faces glared at us through the darkness. They weren't going to be of any help at all, their general comments amid howls of laughter being 'What's the matter Percy, didn't you like the door we'd already got?'

To them it was one huge joke, but to us it was the end of the world. It was the Bloody Tower, Traitors Gate, the firing squad or the Siberian salt mines all rolled into one. But worst of all, too awful to even contemplate, it meant a trip to see 'God' in his Heaven at Derby. We shuddered at the thought. We'd sooner have spent a night with 'Big Bessie', the bone-crusher. We turned pale, hoping the ground would open up and swallow us.

That was until Sam Tweedle, our saviour, turned up. He was better known as 'Pegleg Sam', due to his having one leg and a swinger through attempting to argue with an engine one dark and lonely night.

Sam was our night foreman and he was so old that nothing seemed to surprise him. He'd lived through fire, flood and earthquake. He'd fought in the trenches in World War One killing Germans by the thousand, so the story went, and if anyone could save us from this bloody mess it was Sam.

He started issuing orders, his white moustache bristling. In this mood he reminded me of General Kitchener pointing from the poster: 'Your Country Needs You!' But in our opinion nobody in the world could save us, we were doomed. What we sorely needed was divine intervention.

Dick Turpin, our chief fitter, was first instructed to go and find a steel hawser. The rest of the staff were told to clear off and laugh their silly heads off somewhere else. Poor old Percy, still shaking like a virgin in a brothel, was ordered to bring the offending Class '8', 8123, as far down the bay as possible.

'And don't bring it through the bloody hole this time,' Sam bellowed, 'or you'll have the whole bloody Loco down about our ears!'

'What's the drill, Sam?' I asked hesitantly.

'Well, with a bit of luck and a steady pull, once we've fastened the hawser to your escaped engine, we might, I repeat, just might, manage to pull her back through the same hole she went out of. It's worth a try anyway.'

He broke off to shout orders to the fitter.

'That's it, Dick, fasten it round the coupling and make sure it's tight - it's got 80 ton to pull, so stand well clear.'

He then turned his attentions to Percy.

'Now you, Percy - put your sands on to make certain she doesn't slip. When you've taken up the slack I want a steady pull and for God's sake don't stop until I tell you, got it?'

Percy saluted. 'Yes, Sam. Anything you say, Sam.'

'Right, take the strain,' Sam commanded as the hawser began to creak and groan. 'Steady now. Right, go, go, go!'

Slowly, inch by inch, 8132 eased forward. 'Keep her going,' 'General Kitchener' urged, tapping his gammy leg with a steel ruler. As I peered through the darkness with bloodshot eyes, Sam seemed to be dressed in a khaki uniform with red tabs on the shoulders, a peaked cap complete with red flash, highly polished riding boots, a monocle and a Sam Brown belt with twin Colt revolvers. . .

'I wonder if he'll shoot poor old Percy,' I mused. 'Hope not - he's likely to get mobbed by hordes of screaming frustrated women if he does. . .'

'Jack, wake up!' Sam shouted at me, 'Go outside and keep an eye on your blasted engine. Tell me if it's pulling true.'

'OK, Sam. If she's willing to pop back into her stable I'll give you the thumbs up.'

I ran back outside, but 3772 was digging her heels in as though reluctant to go back where she'd just barged out from. But even she, stubborn as she was, couldn't compete with a mighty Class '8'. So back she came, grumbling, complaining and groaning. She followed to absolute perfection the ruts she had ploughed across the yard, then her tender eased slowly through the silhouette in the wall. When she reached the track, Sam shouted to Percy to stop, then went down on his one good knee to make certain she'd remount the rails she'd been so eager to leave.

'My God, that's a bit of luck,' he chortled. 'She's spot on to the inch. Right Percy, slowly forward.'

Bump. Her first set of wheels went over the flattened stops, then the next, then the next.

'She's OK, Sam,' I yelled as I watched the chimney. I could hardly believe my eyes - she slotted through the hole she'd made on the outward journey to the inch. Bump. On went her last pair of wheels, and she was home.

There was a great cheer, plus a lot of cap waving and applause from the assembled crowd. You'd think we'd just launched a battleship in Tyneside instead of just pulling an engine back on the rails.

'Good old Percy,' they cried. 'When are you going to do it again?'

His reply is unprintable. Suffice it to say that it was extremely unlikely he would ever get the chance to do it again. The powers that be, in their wisdom, came to the decision that we were far too dangerous to remain within the environs of their precious Loco. It was ordered that, forthwith, we were to stay out on the main line, and let the unwary passengers take their chances with us.

But the last chapter on this night's work was to be written by Sam, and it wiped the smirk off the faces of everyone who hadn't had the good sense to clear off while the going was good. He set about organising the unwilling participants into gangs of four.

'You lot collect the bricks, you lot clean them off, and you lot start mixing the cement.'

He stopped issuing orders, looked round and saw the dark figure huddling to make itself inconspicuous in the shadows.

'You!' he yelled, pointing at Billy Blinkhorn, 'Bill the Brick. You're in charge of the bricklaying, so go and round up anyone who's ever laid a brick in their lives and get them cracking. Before dawn breaks I want this wall put back together again. In fact I want it putting back as fast as Percy knocked it down. Now don't forget, you're in charge.'

This made Billy feel quite important, so much so that he puffed out his weedy little chest and started issuing instructions.

'Well,' he strutted about, 'I've never been a boss before, but I could get quite used to the idea. You do this,' he snapped, 'you do that. Come on, you idle lot.'

He quite fancied himself, did Billy, that is until somebody threw a brick at him while Sam's back was turned. Billy retreated up on to the footplate of 3772 where the rabble couldn't get to him. Somehow, God only knows, the bricks were all put back into place and everyone sworn to secrecy. This avoided the necessity of reporting the incident to 'God's minions' but, more importantly, it avoided the need for us to go and see 'God' himself.

No one would have been the wiser as to what had happened that night had it not been for one small item. An item that only made itself visible when daylight finally came. All the sooty bricks that had been on the inside, and all the whitewashed bricks that had been on the outside, had now swapped places.

Outside the Loco, in sharp contrast silhouetted against the beautifully whitewashed wall, was the perfect replica, in sooty black, of an LMS Class '3' freight engine. And inside the Loco, the reverse had happened. On our beautiful black grimy wall, picked out in a delicate shade of best quality whitewash, was the same bloody engine!

This was due to one of Bill the Brick's brilliant brainwaves. He had worked it out in his tiny brain. Seeing as his inexperienced labourers were toiling away in the dark and gloomy confines of the Loco, he thought they would make a better job of piecing the wall back together if they slotted the pure white bricks into the gaps left by the sooty ones. A smashing idea - it showed clear thinking and initiative. Until, in the clear light of the sun, we had all trooped outside to admire his handiwork.

'Come here you little perisher!' Sam yelled after Billy's retreating figure. 'If I get hold of you I'll break you into pieces and stuff you in the bloody firebox!'

But no chance. Billy had scurried off to the comparative safety of the welcoming arms of 'Big Bessy'. I think even God himself would have done a runner if faced by the massive frame of 'Big Bessy'. To add insult to injury, some wag had purloined the whitewash bucket and painted on the sooty bricks outside, for all the world to see, the number of our runaway engine, 3772, and underneath the words: 'Percy's Private Entrance'. Sam swore he would personally castrate the culprit if he laid hands on him, but he never did. We all had our suspicions that it was Bill the Brick's handiwork, but no, he swore, he couldn't write, had never learned.

The book therefore had to be closed on this chapter of Percy's life.

But he damn well soon opened the book again to start a new chapter once we got back on to passenger duties. He was up to his old tricks regarding he fairer sex in no time at all, until one day he almost met his Waterloo.

On this particular night he had slipped into the coaches, as was his habit, to give succour and comfort to a young blonde he had discovered sat all alone in the first compartment, and they were getting on famously.

Until, suddenly, just when he thought he'd cracked it, who should stroll back into the carriage but the said lady's six-foot-three husband who, having downed a few pints, had decided to pay a visit to the station toilet.

He took one look at Percy, who had the nubile young lady in what can best be described as a half-Nelson, let out a great bellow of rage, then thumped poor old Percy one right in the eye. Percy, quite naturally, beat a hasty retreat, loudly proclaiming his innocence and that all he was attempting to do was revive the distressed young lady by giving her mouth-to-mouth resuscitation. He then threw himself headlong down on to the track and sneaked aboard the engine, slamming the cab doors behind him. He hid in the coal bunker while the demented husband tore up and down the platform swearing blue murder if he got hold of the would-be Lothario who had just attacked his sweet and hitherto untouched young lady wife!

In his mad pursuit the deranged fellow even poked his head over the cab doors, but Percy was too well hidden in the nutty slack. I caught a glimpse of the lady in question whilst her husband was charging up and down the platform like a mad bull, and she was laughing her socks off. 'If she's sweet and innocent, I'll eat my hat,' I grinned. Even so, for the next fortnight Percy was swanning around pretending to be a famous film star, hiding behind an enormous pair of dark glasses to cover up his black eye!

And that was the end of my sojourn with the renowned Percy, thank God, for as I explained earlier, it wore me out just watching him.

Well, almost the end. There was just one more incident. Nothing unusual for Percy, really, only that due to his insatiable curiosity he almost fell off a viaduct. It was our last week's work together and we had just manned a special passenger train up the Nottingham bank to Mansfield, arriving at twelve midnight.

Now, the normal drill after emptying the train would be to shunt the coaches back into the carriage sidings set aside for them. But as this was a special, no provision had been made to accommodate it, the sidings being already crammed full with coaches that were due out first thing Monday morning. The 'bobby' at Mansfield Station North advised us to carry on down the line for a further 300 yards, and as soon as we had cleared the points he'd pull off the signal that protected number 3 platform, thus enabling us to reverse into this little-used bay. So off we set along the giant viaduct that carried our main line over the built-up area of Mansfield. The guard was on my side of the engine and immediately I spotted his red light that told us we had cleared the points I called out to Percy to stop.

We stopped all right. A hundred feet up in the air, but only ten feet away from the bedroom window of the flat above a bank. Now, in normal circumstances this bedroom would have been very private indeed, for all the trains that went by would have been speeding along at 40 miles per hour. And just think of it, where could you get that was more private than the highest flat in Mansfield? Well, it was private until fate took a hand and allowed Percy an uninterrupted view of the goings-on in this most private of boudoirs.

And boy, of boy, what goings on there were! The gentleman in question was tall, plump, handsome, and as naked as the day he was born. He was busily chasing a quite energetic young lady round and round. She was dressed in a baby-doll nightie that left nothing to the imagination. She couldn't have been a day over twenty, and if she had popped into the bank that night for a quick deposit she was certainly about to get it. At that vital moment he caught up with her - well, she wasn't running that fast anyway, so she didn't take much catching. He then threw her on the bed amidst great confusion and followed her by executing a swallow dive.

Needless to say, Percy became so excited that he stepped off the engine on to the viaduct to obtain a better view, and almost emulated the acrobatics of the said naked gentleman by copying his swallow dive. The one big difference was that Percy would not have received such a warm welcome on landing, just a considerable drop on to the solid, uncompromising concrete road below. Still, not a bad way to end things as far as Percy was concerned, you might think. He would certainly had departed this earth with a happy smile on his face.

We were still there, with our faces glued to the window, half an hour later when Joe Lyons, our guard, having got sick of hanging out of his van waving his green lamp in vain, came huffing and puffing down the line to find out what was stopping the job.

'What the hell's gone wrong?' he shouted. 'You're stopping the bloody LMS Railway from functioning!'

'Damn the bloody LMS Railway,' Percy whispered back, 'and keep your bloody voice down. Nip up here Joe and feast your eyes on this.'

Percy's precarious perch - Mansfield Viaduct in 1990. *Author*

Joe climbed up on the engine and looked through the bedroom window.

'My God,' he gasped. 'The last time I went in that mean bugger's bank for a loan I couldn't get a sausage out of him.'

'Well she bloody well is,' Percy grinned, 'and if I was him she'd be getting another!'

After a further twenty minutes the sig-nalman, anxious to get home for his Saturday night fish and chips and whatever else might follow if he was lucky, came to the decision that the only way he could get the LMS Railway to start operations again was to blow his hunting horn. This could be guaranteed to wake the dead, and wake the dead it did judging by the state the portly naked gentleman was in after baby-doll had finished with him. Somehow, though, he did manage to rouse himself on hearing the permanent way look-out's hunting horn, no doubt thinking it was the call to arms, or the bank was on fire. He heaved himself off the casting couch, rushed across to the window, and came eye-ball to eyeball with the three white faces staring directly into the bedroom. He let out a great screech and yanked the curtains across.

'Ah,' we all sighed. 'What a shame - and we were all enjoying it as much as you were.'

This caused him to poke his head through the window. 'Clear off you nosy buggers!' he screamed. 'I'll have the authorities on you lot, you mark my words!'

Taking a well-deserved holiday after the trials of being booked with 'Passionate Percy' - myself in 1946. *Author*

But Percy had the last word.

'Sure, but don't forget to tell them where you left your final deposit,' he laughed.

12

CONTROL GET THEIR FEET WET

In 1947, after completing my six months with Percy, I was booked with a much more sober-minded driver by the name of Bill Johnstone; and his sober mind was put severely to the test during our first few weeks together.

In contrast to the many pleasant memories I have of the spring and summer of that year was the dreadfully severe winter that caught everyone unawares. We were really thrown in at the deep end.

The exceptionally bad weather didn't last many weeks, but the snow and floods brought absolute chaos to the operation of the railways. And it was one of the very few times when we were able to have the last laugh over the bowler-hat brigade. It was their collective duty to walk in front of our passenger trains dressed in thigh boots and plunge their hands into the freezing water to feel the points, literally, with their fingers.

Block telegraph and electrical installations were totally useless under two feet of water, and to become de-railed in these conditions would have been catastrophic, with no chance of the giant steam cranes being able to leave the safe confines of the loco yard. The floods in Nottingham stretched from Lenton South Box, two miles distant from the station, right into Nottingham Midland Station itself, where, due to the rise of the line as it reached out to London Road Junction, the swirling waters covered three-quarters of the platforms.

So, for the full extent of the two miles into the station, one of the bowler-hatted Inspectors was detailed to meet each passenger train as it approached from the north,

wave a red flag by day, or a red light at night, and inform the train crew to follow him at walking pace. Also to be prepared to stop immediately if he gave a warning signal.

Once or twice the Inspectors were seen to lose their footing and part wade or swim in their desperate search for the vital points. Up on the footplate, in comparative warmth and safety, we would be falling about laughing at their antics. Luckily for us, over a period of two weeks the constant level of the flood water stopped just six inches below the level of our fires. Provided we kept the dampers shut and proceeded with caution, we were just out of trouble. But if the floods had risen just that vital six inches, Nottingham would have been completely cut off from the outside world, and the knock-on effect regarding passenger, goods and coal trains would have been disastrous.

All these problems had been caused by the River Trent bursting its banks along the whole of its reaches through Nottinghamshire, but the densely populated low-lying Meadows area and the railway system were the worst effected.

Meanwhile, to the north of Nottingham, in my home town of Mansfield, the difficulty was of a different nature. Although there was only a fifteen-mile gap between the two, it was like entering a new world. Up there the snow hadn't melted, but remained in drifts up to eight feet high, and the freezing wind could, and did, alter the whole pattern of the landscape within minutes. As soon as a crew of gangers cleared a path, the howling wind would pile the snow in another spot. Here, the points weren't flooded, they were frozen

Radford Station, just north of Lenton, during the floods of 1947. *Nottingham Evening Post*

If the floods had risen just another six inches, Nottingham would have been cut off from the outside world. A view of the Midland Station during the 1947 floods. *Nottingham Evening Post*

solid and the platelayers had to be constantly at the ready with buckets of salt whenever the signalmen reported that their levers had gone solid.

I remember vividly one such bitterly cold night in particular when we were working the 9.10 pm from Nottingham to Worksop. We didn't just encounter one near impossible situation, but several on the trot, each one confronting us the further we travelled north. A journey that should have taken a maximum of 1 hour 45 minutes lengthened out to a freezing five hours before we reached the safety of Worksop Station.

First we had to crawl through the floods in Nottingham. Having cleared them, when we arrived at Hucknall, seven miles distant, the points had frozen so solid that the salt was having no effect on them whatsoever. However, four or five shovels of our white hot fire did the trick.

But the drama was still to come. We were OK through Mansfield and down the six-mile stretch to Shirebrook, but there we stood, and looked like we would remain standing, 300 passengers or not. The 'bobby'

informed us that between there and Langwith a cutting two miles long was blocked solid with the drifting snow.

'Unless you're prepared to give it a try,' he suggested hesitantly, 'I'm afraid the passengers are stranded here for the night.'

Their cold white faces made the decision for us. Like us, they'd had enough. All they wanted was to get home to their loved ones and a warm fire. My mate Bill Johnstone said grimly 'We'll take a chance. If we don't we'll freeze to death if we stop here.'

He shouted down to the porter to warn the passengers to keep their heads in and the windows tightly shut. Not much chance of them popping their heads out anyway with ice a foot long hanging from the carriage roofs and the windows frozen solid. This was despite the fact that I had the steam heating for the coaches hovering around the red danger mark of 50 lbs instead of the more normal 30 lbs, and still couldn't force any steam

Troops were called in to clear the line. Here a train of tankers is snowed in on the main Derby-Nottingham line at Nuthall Junction. *Nottingham Evening Post*

through the carriage couplings, so solidly frozen were they.

Bill next asked permission from the 'bobby' to reverse the train a couple of hundred yards back up the line in order to get a run at it.

'Keep her blowing off, Jack - we're going to need all the power she can give us.'

Lucky for us, instead of the normal passenger engine with its large wheels built for speed, the loco foreman, in his wisdom, had decided to detail one of our 'maid of all work' engines, a Class '4' freight, No 4394, for this day's work. Much smaller driving wheels, nowhere near as fast, but a damn sight more powerful. I already had a white hot fire on, so all it needed was topping up. 'Bang' went both safety valves. Bill snapped on the steam sanders to give us maximum grip, then opened her up.

'Hang on, Jack,' he shouted. 'Don't know what's facing us round the corner. . .'

Driver Joe Blatherwick and 'Blondie'. They had 4394 the day after we blasted through the snow drift at Shirebrook. *'Blondie' Hurt*

As matters turned out it was a damned good job we didn't - I don't think that we would have attempted it otherwise. The only clue we had regarding what might lay ahead was the slight glimpse we'd had as we stood on the end of the platform before reversing. From there the line to Shirebrook and Langwith curves sharply to the left, and all we could see was the first thirty yards or so before it disappeared out of sight. The line was buried under at least a couple of feet of snow and that was enough to convince us that this was going to be no easy ride. As we again approached the end of the platform, this time pushing 30 miles per hour and accelerating, we looked fearfully through our windows.

The solid white wall of snow looked impregnable. I honestly think we would never have made it if the line had not curved the way it did. The tight left-hand bend had the effect of making 4394 act like a snowplough. She didn't pile it up in front of her but tended to push it away to the right of her, like a scythe. Nonetheless, as we hit the deep drift head-on snow completely enveloped us on the open footplate, and as much as she

began to dig her heels in, 4394 began to falter and rock slightly. There was no danger of becoming de-railed - even this hard wedge of solid snow couldn't lift eighty tons - but even so we had a few heart-stopping moments before the white mist began to clear. Suddenly, like a cork coming out of a bottle, we leapt clear, and Langwith Station came into view.

Bill grinned across at me. 'You look more like a snowman than a fireman, Jack.'

We laughed as we looked at ourselves. The snow had transformed our sober black uniforms into Snow White outfits - all we needed then was for the Seven Dwarfs to show up. Even our beautiful black mountain of coal looked like an alpine ski-slope.

Somehow, against all the odds, we had made it, and were the passengers relieved! They even gave us a cheery wave and a shouted 'Thank you' as they piled out at their respective stations. At long last we pulled into Worksop and unloaded the remainder of the passengers.

But for us the worst was still to come. We had now got to struggle back through the snow to Mansfield. We hadn't sufficient time left to run round the triangle at Shireoaks in order to be chimney-first, so, perish the thought, we had to face it tender-first.

I put a damned good fire on to carry us over the heavy bank between Worksop and Whitwell, then we fastened up the tarpaulin between engine and tender, which would at least give us some protection. Then, having donned scarves and overcoats, off we set. It was the coldest ride I've ever experienced in my life. By the time we reached Langwith we were frozen solid, and we still had to plough through the snow in the cutting!

Bill told the 'bobby' at the station box that we were stopping for a few minutes while we thawed out. I promptly flung open the firebox doors, and boy, oh boy, was that fire welcome!

'Right, that's it Jack,' Bill called out. 'We've got the road so hang on, we'll have a run at it.'

After several traumatic weeks, the weather began to relax its icy grip. A snow scene at Nottingham Midland Station, winter 1947. *Nottingham Evening Post*

'Run at it' was the operative phrase. We went hell for leather through that cutting with both of us ducked under the lip of the tender to get what cover we could, and within ten minutes, with the snow bombarding us like an avalanche, we were through.

By God, were we glad to see Mansfield! It took an hour hard up against the messroom fire and a couple of brew-ups before we thawed out and felt anything like normal.

Eventually, after several traumatic weeks, the winter did begin to relax its icy grip on the surrounding countryside. The deep snow and ice in and around Mansfield began to lessen and the dreadful flood-waters in Nottingham began to recede. The boats that had been manned by the local police to ferry people around the low-lying areas of West Bridgford and the Meadows were put away for their more normal summer pursuits as pleasure cruisers up and down the River Trent.

The platelayers stowed their salt away, the gangers their snow shovels, and the bowler-hat brigade their wellingtons and thigh boots. They then started to get their own back for the many laughs we had enjoyed at their expense.

We even started to look forward to Christmas Day around the fireside, if we had any coal to build it up with, and anything much to cook around it. My mate Bill saw to it that we had.

'Leave it to me, Jack,' he promised. 'We'll have something a bit special after what we've put up with this last couple of months.'

And, true to his word, two days before Christmas we struck a bargain. A farmer needed a few lumps of coal for his fire, and we wanted a pair of ducks for the pot.

'Another satisfied customer, eh, Jack?' Bill grinned as he handed over one of the ducks.

Two whole days to ourselves. It was magic, pure bliss. No having to leave a nice warm bed in the early hours of the morning to face the freezing world outside. Nobody on your back when the going got rough. Nobody to harass you into even greater efforts against sometimes seemingly impossible odds. No watching out for distant signals, or howling winds whipping the coal dust into your eyes.

No working against the clock or persuading reluctant engines to steam against their will, or getting wet through then trying to dry out in readiness for a hard day's slog. Yes, pure magic! Bliss!

After a luxurious lie-in, Christmas Day would start by taking our son, David, now eighteen months old, for a walk around the small mining village where we had settled since getting married three years previously. It was the done thing then for all the proud fathers to parade their offspring up and down the village street to show them off and compare. That was until twelve o'clock, opening time. Then it was hot-foot down to the local for a couple of pints and a natter while the wives cooked the dinners. But only on the strict understanding that, come nightfall, it was their turn for a treat.

However my Maisie used to manage I'll never know. Just consider for a moment the tools with which she had to work. No such luxuries as electric or gas ovens in our row of cottages. Just one coal fire, with the oven on one side and the boiler for hot water on the other. In this one tiny oven Maisie cooked not only our normal meals, but baked bread and cakes as well.

But manage somehow she did. Come two o'clock she had turned up trumps. Roast duck, baked potatoes, sprouts from the garden, stuffing made from chestnuts from the nearby woods, and beautifully cooked Christmas pudding. More pudding than currants, but beggars can't be choosers. Yes, she did well, did Maisie. She was a good lass then, and still is forty years on, bless her. It was damned hard work for a woman in those days. It was bad enough for us men, but they had it harder - I take my hat off to them.

The Christmas of '47 was particularly difficult for Mais', for we were within hours, literally, of expecting our second child. We had hoped against hope that she would be born on Christmas Day, but we were denied this by four days.

Kathy took her first look at this hard world on 29 December, and hard it was by today's standards. It may only be forty-odd years past, well within living memory, but in those days you learned to fight for yourself, stand on your own two feet and not be beholden to anyone. No state handouts that you hadn't worked for, apart from five shillings a week family allowance which you only received for the second child. Candles and oil-lamps were the order of the day, there being only one gaslight in the whole house, and a hot brick wrapped up in a clean sack to take the chill off the bed.

But sheer luxury wasn't far off. Shortly after Christmas, having worked two Sundays on the trot, we walked the three miles into Sutton with enough money jingling in Maisie's handbag to treat ourselves to a double gas-ring! We purchased it, and enough rubber tubing to connect it to the gas supply, after a lot of bargaining between Maisie and the shop manager, for the princely sum of £2 10s. We set off with our prized possession, broke again, but happy.

I soon managed to persuade Sam, our next door neighbour, to fit it all together for a couple of pints and, oh, the sheer bliss of being able to boil a kettle for a mug of tea without having to rake out and clean and light the fire.

When you stop for a moment to analyse these small insignificant events, doesn't it sound strange in this day and age to refer to such mundane matters as luxuries? And no, I'm not talking about 1847, I'm talking about 1947.

To the younger generation this must read like I'm talking of another world. By contrast, today we can step on to a jet plane and be whisked off to savour the delights of the world in a matter of hours, or sail away on an ocean liner where unbelievable luxury is the norm. Television, hi-fi's, cars in abundance, meals out in restaurants, fitted kitchens where every convenience is to hand, washing machines, fridges, freezers, vacuum cleaners, fitted carpets, telephones - the list is almost endless. Just think about it, at the flick of a switch today's housewife has the world at her finger-tips. What a marvellous contrast.

Oh, I know you don't think about these things as being yours as a right, but in the days I am remembering it was normal to have none of them! OK, you might consider that we were poor, even stony broke then. Well,

Waiting for dad to come home - David and Kathleen Backen aged 4 and 2½ in 1948. *Author*

The doting grandfather - 'Darky' Backen and granddaughter Kathleen in about 1952. *Author*

THE LONDON MIDLAND AND SCOTTISH RAILWAY SAVINGS BANK.   E.R.O. .1735

T 14248 In Account with **Allan, John Backen.**

Date	Amount in Words at Length.	Amount.	Initials of Receiver of Deposits.	Date	Amount in Words at Length.	Amount.	Initials of Receiver of Deposits.
Dec 29	Deductions through Pay Bills	15			Brought forward		
		69					
Oct. 31	Deductions through Pay Bills	1 4					
	Interest for year						
1st Nov. 1946 Balance.		70 4					
		13					
		6 3					
Oct. 31	Deductions through Pay Bills	20 11 7					
	INTEREST FOR YEAR						
1ST. NOV. 1947 BALANCE.		13 5					
Oct. 31	Deductions through Pay Bills	16 4					
	INTEREST FOR YEAR						
1ST. NOV. 1948 BALANCE.		34 18 11					
1948/9	Deductions through Pay Bills	13					
	Salaries to Octr. 6th.						
	Wages ,, ,, 29th.						
	INTEREST FOR YEAR	1 8					
1ST. NOV. 1949 BALANCE.		49 11					
May 12	W/d	14 0 0					
		35 0 11					
	Carried forward				Carried forward		

My LMS Savings Bank passbook. The last withdrawal recorded, £14, doesn't sound much, but it was nearly three weeks wages then. *Author*

just about everybody I ever knew was stony broke as well. That, too, was the norm. There was nothing unusual in this. For a couple of days or more before pay-day we wouldn't have a single penny in our pockets, but then neither did anyone else.

Compare your today with my yesterday. One coal fire. No electricity. One cold water tap dripping over a stone sink. One lone gaslight to illuminate the dark winter nights. Just imagine trying to bring up two babies in these conditions. Impossible, you say? It's not. We did it, and hundreds of thousands like us. And not only brought them up, but gave them honest values to live by, a sense of right and wrong, a sense of the fitness of things, and a deep conviction that it was our duty to make them into decent members of society.

If you stopped to allow yourself to think, life at the time seemed totally unfair. But you didn't think, you just got on with it and hoped that life would eventually deal you a better hand. But looking back, I wouldn't have swapped it. Your thoughts were for your fellow man. Was he in trouble? Could you help? If he was and you could, then, somehow, you did.

I'm sure my yesterdays built my character - they certainly built humility. No matter how hard up you were, if you looked hard enough, and cared enough, you could always find someone a little worse off than yourself. No, I'm not talking mealy-mouthed platitudes - that was life!

13
A CHRISTMAS TO REMEMBER

I had to remain on passenger work for a further eighteen months. As I have explained, the railway system ran on the strict rule of seniority, which meant that you had to wait for men to retire or die before you could be promoted - or, in railway parlance, to be 'nobbed up'.

Although passenger trains were undoubtedly the glamour side of life on the footplate, the drawbacks far outweighed the advantages. You would find yourself rushing about all over the place like someone not right in the head, and five minutes late could mean a report. On freight trains you could get lost for twenty-four hours at a time and no one would even question it.

The most important aspect of the changeover back to freight, as far as I was concerned, was financial. By this time our two children, David and Kathleen, were needing school clothes and instead of being

Life was nowhere near as hectic firing on freight trains as on passenger duties. Here the fireman has time to admire the view as his mineral train eases out of Nottingham Victoria behind a Class '9' 2-10-0. *Mac Johnstone*

tied down to a strict wage of £5 10s per week, the wages in my tin could vary between £7 and £12. I must admit that I missed the life and the colour that crowds of passengers brought into what was often a boring life, but the boredom was really the only drawback. Everything else was a plus.

The first driver I was booked with in the freight links was Joe Davis. Again I was fortunate in the luck of the draw, for Joe was a man with a ready sense of humour, not to be underestimated when you consider we were to spend the whole year together. We had many interesting and varied weeks' work in our link, mainly coal trains which by their very nature were slow, but we did have the odd express to break up the monotony. It took me quite a long time to re-adjust to the pace of the mainly loose-coupled trains. You daren't whip along very fast with this type of train for fear of being unable to stop in time.

But after I'd adjusted to the pace it was money for old rope. Unless you happened to be working along heavy gradients, the drill adopted was to put on a nice fire, just right for mashing and toasting your sandwiches, then sit back and forget it for a couple of hours. What a pleasant change from never being able to put the firing shovel away! We even had enough time to enjoy a fry-up in place of the usual dried-up sandwiches. There was nothing in the world that could quite compare with the aroma of bacon, sausages, eggs, fried bread and dip sizzling away on a steam-cleaned fireman's shovel strategically placed on the lip of the firebox.

There was only one drawback when preparing this culinary delight. On the odd occasion your driver would forget that you were trying to emulate Fanny Craddock with a shovel, and he would whip the regulator right across. This would not only put a tragic end to your breakfast, sucked into the firebox by the resultant blast, but your shovel as well, which went with it. All you were left with was the smell of a breakfast not-to-be lingering around the chimney end.

Joe was, according to most railwaymen, perfectly normal - like most footplate staff he enjoyed more than his fair share of the three vices that seemed to beset us all. I think they used to turn these drivers out in a mould - they couldn't have been born in the normal way like ordinary mortals. Joe's greatest vice, however, wasn't baccy, or women. It was beer.

We were able to put this besetting sin to the test one day when we were on the Bilsthorpe run. It was Christmas Eve and snowing quite heavily. We had to haul a train of empty wagons to the colliery, shunt them in, then bring out the loaded ones. We were standing at the water column topping the engine up, and as I climbed across the tender towards the water crane I happened to notice that the first wagon attached to our engine was partially sheeted over by a tarpaulin. I thought this rather strange because the wagon was supposed to be empty.

Nobody sheets down an empty waggon. Jumping down off the tender onto the wagon, I lifted the sheet and could hardly believe what I saw. I shouted down to Joe.

'Don't move yet! I've just discovered a bloody gold mine.'

'What the hell are you on about?' he yelled back.

'You'll soon see, as soon as I've let the wagon door down,' I shouted back excitedly.

Nothing untoward could be seen from outside the wagon, but as Joe jumped down off the engine I let the door slam down.

'Eu-bloody-reka!' he cried. 'I don't believe it! Santa, I take it all back, you are real - thank you - oh, thank you!'

There, in all its glory, stood a 45-gallon barrel of beer. Best Bitter.

Joe was into the wagon like lightning - I've never seen him move so fast. He just stood there with his eyes popping out like chapel hat-pegs, rubbing his hands with glee, saying,

'Leave this to me, I have a way with barrels of beer.'

And, sure enough, he did. It was like watching an expert at work. The barrel was far to heavy to manoeuvre, so Joe proceeded to knock in the bung, then inserted one of our spare gauge glasses. After one very large sample, and formally declaring it to be the real thing, he began to suck up the beer through the glass in a brown frothy stream. He carried on sucking for about five minutes without stopping to draw breath. He was turning crimson, and I stood there waiting for him to burst. He stopped at last, and leaned back on the barrel with a look of pure delight on his face. It was my turn next.

I could well understand his ecstasy. It was the finest iced beer I had ever tasted in my life, free or not.

Bill Herrin, our guard, a short, fat, roly-poly man, and a notorious beer drinker, huffed and puffed his way right back down the train to find out why we'd both done a disappearing act after trying to call us back for twenty minutes. Of course, we had been far too pre-occupied with our Christmas present. When his beady little eyes spotted the find in the wagon, this glorious, big, fat barrel, and saw all that beautiful beer going up the glass and down Joe's throat, he was having kittens. Due to his short rotund stature he just could not lift himself, no matter how hard he tried, up on to the wagon.

There was, however, no way we were going to assist him until we'd had our fill, and not then until we'd filled two buckets that I'd steam cleaned. Then, and only then, did we give him a leg up. He immediately seized the gauge glass and proceeded to attack the barrel with such gusto that I even think he surpassed Joe's efforts. Had breathalysers been around in those days, and had we been tested, there would have been no doubt as to the

result. In fact, the result would have been the same if we had been tested a couple of days later!

By the time we got around to doing the job we had come to do, Joe and Bill were really Brahms and Liszt. Being the least effected of the three, I was delegated to do the driving, and the firing, and the guard's duties for the rest of the shift, while the other two slept it off in the guard's van.

Boy, what a Christmas Eve!

While we are in this area another amusing incident comes to mind. There were still quite a few woman employed on the signals, mainly in out-of-the-way signal boxes, and there was one by the name of Lucy. She had been given the name 'Juicy Lucy' by the train crews that worked this section, and not without good reason. Normally, it was always the fireman's duty to proceed forward to the signal box to report in when brought to a halt at a signal, but none of the drivers would allow you to perform this operation at Lucy's box - they all went themselves.

The firemen concerned all knew the reason why, but, the driver being the boss, there was nothing we could do about it. It didn't apply to all the drivers, only most of them, and the procedure was generally the same. No sooner had the driver disappeared inside the signal box when down would go the

Juicy Lucy's casting couch! *Author*

lights and the curtains would be drawn across.

Everything then stood for about an hour until the driver re-appeared. Obviously this caper couldn't continue for too long without questions being asked by one of 'God's minions' and, sure enough, a signals Inspector was duly despatched to find out the reason for the LMS Railway ceasing to function in this area, and deal with the situation forthwith.

Joe and I were detailed to take this member of the dreaded bowler-hat brigade from Mansfield to the offending signal box. After arriving there, the Inspector climbed down from the footplate and, marching with all the authority he could muster, mounted the steps and disappeared inside. Within five minutes down went the lights, across went the curtains.

We waited a full two hours before the Inspector re-appeared in a rather dishevelled state, marched back up to the engine steps, then announced in a voice just a little too loud to carry any real conviction, 'All the rumours about the lady in question are malicious and unfounded. Anyone found to be guilty of spreading more stories about Juicy - er - the lady in question will be dealt with personally!'

Needless to say, life at the box went on in much the same way in future months as it had in the past. Apart from an occasional visit from our Inspector to ensure that all was running smoothly, Lucy's light continued to go on and off like a Belisha beacon for as long as I can remember.

I certainly drew the short straw when it next came to the re-location of drivers after my happy year's stint with Joe Davis. I was paired with a fiery Welshman by the name of Taffy Williams. Most people you meet in life are a compromise between right and wrong, belligerent disposition or placid temperament.

Not Taffy. He was always right, even when he was wrong, which, according to him, he never was. He had a great crop of unmanageable hair which gave him the appearance of a Welsh mountain goat let loose among a herd of nubile nannies. His bat-like ears stuck out

of his bullet-shaped head at such an alarming angle that I was convinced that one day, given the right flying conditions, he would take off just like a jet plane. The only things likely to keep him on terra firma were the size 12 boots he constantly stomped around in. They reminded me of two great anchors put out to keep the *Queen Mary* from drifting.

But the worst thing I had to contend with was his temper. He never spoke, he always shouted. His face never radiated a calm expression, he always looked as though he was about to burst a blood vessel. He was irascible, impatient and wild-eyed. When trying to prove a point they almost popped out of his skull. To emphasise a point he was making he would fling his arms out in every direction and when in full song everybody moved their mugs of tea well out of his way.

In any conversation Taffy always had the floor to himself. There just wasn't room for anyone else as well.

'My God,' I groaned. 'I'm stuck with him for a whole year!'

Taffy was a no-nonsense man. Everything was either black or white, never any shade of grey. I'm certain that it was this wham-bang attitude towards life spilling over to his handling of an engine that caused utter catastrophe one night about six months later.

We were booked on the 11.30 pm block train from Shirebrook to Sheffield with ex-Midland Class '4F' 0-6-0 No 3874. From Cresswell Junction it was a single line and tablet-catching was called for. There was a very steep 1 in 50 uphill gradient to Clowne Station, followed by an equally steep downhill stretch to Seymour Junction, on through Staveley, where you encountered a switchback with an alarming dip in the middle of the line, and, finally, on to the London-Scotland main line at Foxloe Junction where a set of 'Jack points' had been installed to derail you if you ran past the protective stop signal.

The line to Cresswell was straightforward enough, but from there on matters became increasingly more difficult. As you ran past the siding where the banker engine stood, the drill was to shout out at the top of your voice to make certain you had been heard, then go hell for leather to gain as much speed as possible before the gradient pulled you back to a halt. You had to make sure you caught the tablet *en route*.

The signalman would then turn out the banker, which was usually a Midland Class '3' or '4' freight engine, to buffer up to the guard's van at the rear. The guard would then couple him up so that he could assist us in stopping the train once we had cleared the bank. Then, with the usual series of piercing whistles to announce all was well, off we would set, regulators wide open on both engines. After a couple of hundred yards of slipping and sliding we would be blasting our way up the bank with a column of white-hot fire coming out of the chimney like it was Bonfire Night. It was utterly useless for the farmers to plant any crops adjacent to the Seymour bank, for we could be relied upon to set them on fire every time we went by.

That was the theory, anyway. On this occasion, having a particularly heavy train behind us, Taffy asked permission from the 'bobby' to back up as far as possible in order to get a good run at the bank. This we did by reversing the whole train across on to the up line. The banker then went past us to the next cross-over points and hooked up.

When both the engines were ready off we set, both drivers giving the engines their head to gain as much speed as possible. The drill for the fireman in such circumstances was to have a pot full of water, blowing off at both safety valves, and a box full of white-hot fire. There would be little chance of firing again for a few minutes - you had enough problems just hanging on. The difficulty was that we had to negotiate the left 'flick' when we re-crossed from the up to the down line, then twenty yards on the bank proper took a steep left-hand turn.

Added to these problems, as though I needed any more, somehow I had to catch the single-line tablet. Believe me, this was no easy task with the engine bucking like a demented bronco, steam blowing back in your face, and the signalman standing as far back as possible when he handed it to you. I can't say that I blamed him really. If I'd been a signalman standing there with the tablet at the ready and an 80-ton monster bearing down on me spitting fire and fury I'd have done a runner and be damned to the tablet.

Class '4F' 0-6-0 No 44081, a development of the original Midland Railway design which became an LMS standard, over 600 being built. It was one of the original batch, (4)3874, that gave Taffy Williams such trouble. *Mac Johnstone*

The only way the fireman could catch it, and you dare not miss or the job came to a standstill, was to kneel on the footplate, hang on to the handrail with one hand and, leaning out to your fullest extent, make a grab with your free hand. More a job for a trapeze artist than a fireman but, somehow, I managed it. This was the signal for the driver to push the regulator hard over and hang on for dear life.

Now, all would have gone to plan if Taffy had been what you might describe as a normal man. But Taffy, being Taffy, was anything but normal. An immediate difficulty in the form of a rain shower presented itself and this made the lines very slippery. No problem, you would have thought, just snap the sands on. The elementary rule, taught from day one, was that you never put the sands on while the engine was still slipping. The practice was to shut off the regulator, wait for her to right herself, then simultaneously snap on the sands and re-open the regulator. A nice smooth action, you would have thought.

But Taffy wasn't smooth. In fact, Taffy was the complete opposite to smooth. Instead of the delicate, synchronised operation it should have been, Taffy behaved like Taffy. He first cursed the engine for slipping, hoping that this would make her behave better, which of course it didn't. This made him even madder, so he cursed her some more, calling her every unmentionable name under the sun. 3874 continued to ignore him and, pretending she wasn't listening to his sweet dulcet tones, carried on slipping.

Taffy then screamed at her, 'Right, bugger you then, this will fix you!'

He then banged on the sands which had an immediate effect. 3874 stopped doing her tango all right, because all hell broke loose. Cra-ash. Ba-ang. The terrific banging and thumping continued with each revolution of the wheels. Ba-ang! Ba-ang!

Taffy looked across at me, eyes popping out of his scarlet face like one of his terrified rabbits. His face then turned a delicate shade of cream cheese, for not only was 3874 telling us that there was something dreadfully wrong with her nether regions, but she was also attempting to throw Taffy off her footplate by rocking violently from side to side.

Then the rhythm of the engine changed. Suddenly 3874 jumped in the air, crashed back on to the rails and continued with the violent banging.

'What the bloody hell's the matter with you?' Taffy screamed as he looked over the side. He was just about to curse her some more when, at last, his bloodshot eyes focused on the cause of all the trouble. He opened his mouth to say something, then promptly shut it. His face had turned green as he frantically pointed for me to look over on my side. I leaned out as far as I could without being thrown off and saw the reason why Taffy was behaving like a whirling Dervish.

We'd broken the bloody side-rods! Six inches thick and three inches wide, solid steel, and we'd broken them off like they were a couple of matchsticks!

Taffy leapt to the centre of the footplate and started waving his arms in the air.

'Stop! Stop, damn you!'

He slammed the regulator off. The trouble with this was that, with two engines going flat out, you don't slow down. You just stop, and the engine at the back of you runs into you like a battering ram. And this is what happened. The poor unsuspecting guard was thrown from one end of his caboose to the other whilst the driver and the fireman on the banker engine had their faces bashed on to the red-hot boiler.

What they called Taffy later was nobody's business. But this wasn't our immediate problem as we climbed down shakily from the footplate to have a look at the damage. The reason for the continuous banging on the catwalk as the wheels rotated became obvious. The side-rod on my side of the engine was broken off at the gradient pin, and the shattered end of it was thumping along the sleepers. God only knows what would have happened if it had broken off in the opposite direction. It could well have speared itself into the sleepers and tipped us helter skelter down the 40-foot bank.

But the banging had come from Taffy's side. His side-rod hadn't broken - it had just bent itself double! It was distorted to such an extent that it had bashed all the steel rivets off the cat-walk as it went round and round.

Taffy was speechless. He just sat on the sleepers, head in hands, occasionally opening his fingers to take a peek at the wrecked engine, hoping that, somehow, it might unwreck itself. But there was no chance. She wouldn't be hauling any more trains for a long while.

The guard came rushing along the track.

'What the flaming hell. . .?' He stopped in his stride when his eyes fell on Taffy's handiwork. 'How did you do that, Taffy?'

Taffy then became Taffy again. I didn't think the self-imposed silence would last very long.

'I didn't do it, you silly buggers!' he yelled, 'She did it!' He pointed an accusing finger up at the boiler of 3874, which seemed to wilt at his ferocity. 'She wouldn't bloody well stop slipping!'

He then started throwing his arms about as he went into graphic detail regarding 3874's refusal to behave herself.

'So I put the bloody sands on didn't I?' he smirked. Without realising that he was admitting it was all his fault anyway, he grinned: 'That made the silly old bugger stop slipping.'

He gave one of the wheels a vicious kick to emphasise the point and promptly bruised his toe which started him off cursing again.

Freddy Jones, the banker driver, said seriously, 'Yes, Taffy, it would.'

Putting a friendly arm round Taffy's shoulders, he led him up the line a few paces out of earshot and began talking earnestly into his ear. After a few minutes they returned with Taffy calmed down somewhat, or as calm as Taffy ever could be. He then proceeded to shout at us.

'Freddy and I have agreed that what we are going to tell everyone, to get us out of this bloody mess, is that the sands weren't working. . .' He looked around him for any possible signs of dissention. There was none forthcoming, so he continued. 'So I instructed Jack to go up the line with his shovel, find any loose sand there was lying about, then to sprinkle it along the line in front of the engine. Unfortunately, we had just reached his line of sand when this silly bugger,' he pointed up at poor old 3874, 'decided to start slipping again and the sudden jolt of meeting Jack's sand line broke the bloody side-rods.'

Oh, I thought to myself, so it wasn't Taffy's fault after all. It was mine, and 3874's. Funny, I should have known that all the time. . .

'OK?' Taffy grinned. 'Everybody agreed?'

We all nodded our agreement. We had no choice. When Taffy yelled at you to agree, if you had any sense at all, you agreed.

'Right, Jack,' he boomed. 'Get your detonators and red flag and proceed up the line towards Clowne. Put one detonator down at a quarter of a mile, one at a half mile and three at three-quarters of a mile not less than ten yards apart.'

'Yes, I know the procedure, Taffy,' I began to explain, 'but don't forget we're on a single line. You've got the tablet, we're protected. The bobby can't let another train down on to us - the line's locked, so I needn't go.'

'Jack!' he screamed, waving his arms in all directions, 'go on up the bloody line and put them bloody detonators where I've bloody well told you to!'

'OK, Taffy, calm down.' I'd sooner have walked ten miles than have Taffy screaming in my ear. You never know, I thought, if I did walk ten miles I might just get out of earshot.

Even so, if I'd had my way I know where I'd have stuffed Taffy's bloody detonators.

And exploded them!

Off I trudged, clipping the detonators down and waving my red flag at all the non-existing ghost trains that were belting up and down this lonely and deserted track. I was still grumbling to myself when I arrived back an hour later to learn that Taffy had gone hot-foot down to the signal box and summoned help from all directions to hopefully get us out of this almighty cock-up.

He had gone to such pains yelling down the telephone at Control - who could have heard him without the use of the instrument anyway, they were only twenty miles off - that they were beginning to think they had a hero on their hands. They were probably already discussing the possibility of pinning a medal on him. I know where I'd have pinned a medal. . .

'You did very well, driver,' the powers that be enthused. 'To stop your engine in such a short distance with no further damage was a remarkable feat of driving and control. You showed exceptional skill. We are indeed indebted to you.'

'Did you hear that, Jack?' Taffy preened himself. 'They're not such a bad lot at Control after all, you know. Oh, I know I've called them silly buggers in the past,' he nodded wisely, 'but they recognise a talented driver when they see one. Now, don't ever let me hear you criticise them again in the future, understand?' he admonished, wagging a grubby finger under my nose.

'No, Taffy, certainly not, Taffy.'

The result of Taffy's persuasive tongue was that within the space of three hours we had a set of gangers, a posse of fitters, a giant steam crane sent post-haste from Nottingham, and a swarm of bowler-hatted brigade gestapo officers to direct operations.

I think, in retrospect, even Taffy could have directed operations better. One of the bowler-hatted brigade, who seemed to be the boss, sent the 100-ton crane one way, and another one, with a slightly smaller bowler, sent it the other. They got the crane driver in such a tizzy he screamed out from his cab at the top of his voice, 'Clear off you silly buggers, I'll manage on my own!'

Anyway, within a matter of four hours they had drawn the train back off poor old 3874, sent a giant Class '8' loaded with fitters up the line where we were still stuck and, somehow, levered our bent and broken side-rods off the wheels. They then hooked us up to a Class '8' and towed us back to the Loco where the fun really started.

Everyone, from the most junior cleaner, any pedestrians that were passing at the time, right up to the senior day foreman and the office cat were regaled by Taffy on how he had saved the great LMS Railway.

Exactly one month later Taffy and I parted company to go our separate ways. No longer to have Taffy yelling in my delicate ear was pure heaven.

14
AN APPOINTMENT WITH 'GOD'

During the spring of 1949 we had two sharp reminders that not only was there a great deal of humour and job satisfaction attached to our chosen profession, but also danger and tragedy as well. They merely reiterated the lessons that had been instilled into us, lessons that, with the passing of time, you tended to shove into the back of your mind - that mentally and physically this was a tough and demanding profession.

One of my firemen friends had just been booked with a driver named Alf Renshaw, a fairly young driver in the same age group as Taffy and Percy. As we were now considered old hands, any special work that was allocated to our depot, even if it meant going back on to passengers for a day or two, we would usually find ourselves assigned to it. And more often than not we would find ourselves driving as much as firing.

On this particular day Alf and his fireman, Cockney, were on one of the Worksop passenger runs. Having shunted the coaches into the sidings, they were running light engine around the triangle at Shireoaks to turn the engine right way round for the return journey. As was usual, they found themselves with very little time to accomplish the many and varied tasks before being due away again. Consequently, Alf was out on the tender pulling down sufficient coal for the trip back when they passed underneath a road bridge. Due to a number of unlucky coincidences slotting together, a dreadful fatality occurred.

Alf was killed instantly through coming into contact with the bridge. This tragedy could never normally have happened, but the safety regulations which should have pre-vented the accident were not observed. Neither Alf nor Cockney, no doubt being pre-occupied, saw the danger. Even so, in ninety-nine cases out of a hundred, with the bridge parapet being two foot above the engine, there would have been enough clearance. For reasons unknown to anyone it was not the case in this instance.

Again, according to the rules no one should be on a tender whilst the engine is in motion, but it was a rule that we, without exception, always broke whenever we were pushed for time. Which was always.

Two weeks after Alf's death we were all shocked by a further tragedy. A driver who was universally liked by both young and old met a similar fate. His name was Bill Turner, and one of the many reasons for his popularity was that he voluntarily sacrificed quite a lot of his free time in order to take classes of young firemen and patiently teach them the intricacies of both the Rule Book and the engineer's black book. He had immense patience with us all, and in his soft, quietly spoken manner would guide us through what seemed to us, initially, seemingly impossible problems.

He must have been suffering from some very deep-seated trouble that he found impossible to overcome, for one day he didn't turn up for work as usual but cycled down to Shirebrook where he knew the trains would be moving too quickly to be stopped. Whether by design or accident, we never knew the answer, he was found lying dead in the middle of the track by a passing engineer.

He must have died instantly, but the ironic part of the story was that it seems likely that he had been struck down by the train he would normally have been driving.

Arthur Wells, the driver with whom I was next booked, and myself had one thing in common - accidents. Whether it was purely coincidental or not I will never know, but one thing I did know - in fact you could guarantee it - was that in the nine months we spent together we would be slap bang in the middle of any pile-ups or runaways that occurred in our neck of the woods. It was certainly not due to lack of skill. Arthur was a very competent driver and with the experience I had amassed over the years I was well on top of my job. Practically all the problems we encountered were along one particular stretch of line that had earned itself a notorious reputation. It was not a long stretch, about 25 miles in all, but what it lacked in miles it more than made up for in contrast. It was that same stretch of track on which Taffy had bent 3874 - from Cresswell through Clowne to Staveley.

Arthur and I used to find ourselves on this stretch of line quite often where we worked the loose-coupled block trains through to Sheffield. On the day shift it was a fairly straightforward run (Taffy notwithstanding!), but on nights it could be a very different story indeed, for more often than not during the winter months the line was totally fog-bound.

We used to sign on at 11.35 pm and travel light engine with the guard down to Shirebrook sidings. There we would hook up to our prepared coal train and usually be loaded down to the hilt. The ascent of the 1 in 50 would - hopefully - follow the procedures already described. Having reached the top, before proceeding on to the steep downhill section, we'd bring the train to a halt at the stop signal with the assistance of the banker engine's brakes to allow the guard to pin down the brakes on every second wagon along the length of the train in order to give us some chance of controlling the heavy load without it running hopelessly away with us, which it always did anyway. It usually took the guard about 45 minutes to complete this task.

This spare time was put to good use. It gave us the chance to draw our breath and the opportunity to put the kettle on and have a leisurely snap-time. This invariably

An early view of the LMS station at Clowne, at the top of the fearsome single-line 1 in 50 bank. *Eric Edwards*

consisted of bread and cheese, a large baked onion which I had lodged on top of the injector some three hours previously, a pinch of salt and several mugs of piping hot tea. Humble fare, certainly, but unless you've experienced feasting off it at three o'clock on a cold winter's morning, you haven't lived!

On receiving the 'right away' from the guard, off we would go again, with the most dangerous stretch still facing us. Having swapped the tablets, thus allowing us into the next section, all was plain sailing, or steaming, for a couple of hundred yards until the weight of the train, about a thousand tons, began to make itself felt. We would then be pushed inexorably forward, faster and faster, even though both the engine and guard's brakes were fully applied. However many times you experienced this it never failed to thrill and frighten you at the same time. With the knowledge that there was absolutely nothing you could do to stop it, this terrible weight would be pressing down on you, pushing you ever onwards, and you knew that if anything went wrong on either the line or the engine there would be one hell of a pile-up. Your only chance of survival would be to jump for it.

This was a situation that many of the train crews experienced, but we were always taught never to take the chance unless the situation was absolutely hopeless - the danger of hitting something in the dark and being thrown back under the churning wheels was too great. I knew one or two footplatemen that had been forced into taking the decision to jump and they'd ended up either dead or legless.

At the bottom of the bank a sharp right-hand curve had been built into the line to assist the driver in bringing the train to a halt. The purpose of the curve was to force both the engine and wagon wheel flanges to bind sharply, thus having a steadying effect on the whole train. For the first time for five miles we were able to bring the train under control, but you could never guarantee this, as I experienced personally, for twice within a month we were forced to whistle up the signalman with a series of long piercing blasts to clear the road ahead for us. Fortunately he was able to do this and turned us into a dead-end siding about a mile in length and curving sharply uphill. This had been specially constructed for the purpose of stopping runaways.

Having finally come to a stand, and after the guard had released his brakes, rather gingerly for they were very hot, the following five miles, after first giving up the tablet for we were now on double track, were fairly straightforward until we reached the dip in the line mentioned previously where you could break the train in two if you weren't careful.

The trick was to keep steam on in order to keep the couplings taut. Not an easy task, for as you were pulling out of the dip on the far side, the wagons at the rear end of the train were still travelling downhill and would begin to buffer up; this always pulled you back with an almighty snatch as the train eventually levelled out. Many has been the time that trains have been broken in this section.

An added difficulty was that you daren't have too much steam on because 300 yards ahead was a stop signal protecting a junction, and it was invariably at danger. In order to gain precious seconds we found that if we laid flat on the footplate the signal would come into view for a split second through the bridge archway. This would allow you just enough time to bring the train to a halt if necessary. If the signal showed green we were OK for half a mile to the next signal, but this was a very important signal, protecting the London-Scotland main line, complete with 'Jack points' to catch the unwary traveller.

I remember this junction vividly. An incident occurred almost a month to the day after being booked with Arthur. We had been struggling with a particularly heavy train and a partially crippled engine for the whole night. The reason the engine was giving us problems was due to the flange packing having blown out one of the pistons, thus wreathing us in clouds of steam that escaped with each stroke of the piston. To make matters worse, we had been driving through a real thick pea-souper of a fog. As we approached the protective signal for the main line my mate shouted for me to keep a sharp look-out as the signal was on my side of the engine, but way overhead at a height of about 20 feet.

In normal circumstances this would have created no great problem, for having driven over this stretch of the line hundreds of times we knew exactly where to locate it. However, this night, with the thick fog and the engine blowing steam across our faces and the need on a greasy line to keep the engine just inching forward, was anything but normal. If we had stopped for any reason there would have been no chance of starting again. The 'bobby', being conversant with the problems, always tried to give us a clear green signal and usually did.

But not this time. He was pulled off clear on his main line for the night 'Scotsman' to come roaring through. Due to the mixture of fog, escaping steam and noise, I neither saw nor heard a thing until, with no hint or warning, we felt the engine jump the rails and bump along the sleepers with the wagons all buffering up to us with an almighty clang that reverberated right down the train to the guard's brake. He informed us later that he had been thrown neck and crop off his seat and dumped unceremoniously on to the floor of his van. It then dawned on us what had happened. We'd run past the signal at danger and had run foul of the 'Jack points', with the inevitable result dreaded by all train crews.

We were off the road. De-railed!

Smoke, steam and thick fog, with a busted piston valve - it's no wonder we were derailed on the jack-points. An '8F' in a similar condition to our '4F'. *D. E. Gouldthorp*

Rule 179, the protection rule, had to be applied immediately. I rushed forward with my red lamp and detonators after first dashing into the signal box to inform the 'bobby' of our position. I also had to make certain that he placed clips on the relevant levers to protect us from any oncoming train on the opposite line, which we were fouling. I then fastened five detonators on to the line at quarter mile intervals with the last three ten yards apart. This was the first line of protection. If any driver that was advancing into our section ran over three detonators he would stop automatically.

I then walked back to see how my mate was faring. It had been his duty to go back and inform the guard who would then protect the train in the rear in the same fashion as I had done at the front. Having completed these tasks, there was nothing more that could be done until the fog lifted and daylight arrived, so we all made our way up into the signal box to hold an inquest. It appeared that the signalman had stood out on his balcony waving a red light and shouting at the top of his voice in an attempt to stop us. Through the wreaths of steam and fog he could hear us but couldn't see us. We had been in a similar position for the same reasons.

It was precisely three o'clock in the morning when we jumped the track, and although Control had been immediately informed, we had to sit it out until eight o'clock when a set of Staveley men were dispatched to relieve us. They came complete with breakdown coach, around twenty platelayers, a couple of the bowler-hatted fraternity and a steam crane for manoeuvring our sad old engine back on to the track.

This operation was not completed until midday, and both the up and down lines had been blocked for twelve hours causing delays and diversions for miles and miles around. We were informed of this after at last reaching our Loco at three o'clock in the afternoon.

Because of the congestion that the de-railment had caused, we were informed that a report had already been despatched to the LMS headquarters at Derby. We were told to report there at nine o'clock the following morning to see 'God'. They issued us with brand new uniforms for the interview which, we were told, would have to be immediately relinquished upon our return. We were allowed a union representative to accompany us into 'God's' office, but for all the good it did us he needn't have bothered. He never uttered a word. I can only imagine that he was too afraid to speak on our behalf, for the governors still held the power of life and death over us.

We were ushered into the room by a secretary and the first thing we saw was a long carpet which seemed to stretch for a mile. It was like walking the plank.

At the end of this carpet an enormous desk was strategically placed, behind which sat four of the governors. The reason for the long carpet was intimidation, of course, and it succeeded. You felt about six inches high by the time you finally reached the end of it.

We were only allowed into their exalted presence separately. Arthur had already been grilled, so it was now my turn.

They fired questions at me one after the other, hardly giving me time to answer before asking others. The final verdict at the end of the interview was that we were both to be severely reprimanded. The only reason we were let off the hook was because of the adverse weather conditions that prevailed at the time, together with the fact that we had been severely hampered by the leaking piston valve. We were then told, in no uncertain manner, not to read anything into these findings, for we would not be shown the leniency if a similar occurrence should happen in the future.

When you stand back and look at the situation as it existed at the time, in all fairness we should not have been blamed for what had happened. But that was the attitude that prevailed in those days. Never would the authorities accept any liability whatsoever for any mishaps that befell you on their rails. Always it was the fault of the employees, even though they were, in the main, conscientious and tried their utmost to overcome events that were very often beyond their control.

I should imagine that I am no exception to the rule when I say that certain isolated experiences that occurred half a life-time ago remain vividly in my memory. To bring them to the fore of one's mind and re-live them is, to say the least, still very distressing.

One such incident took place over the same stretch of line one night in 1950. It was two o'clock in the morning, but a full moon lit up the countryside. We had just left Clowne signal box and, as usual, were progressing extremely slowly to hold the train in check prior to hitting the steep downhill section. We were only crawling along at about 2 miles per hour, and, with the engine being badly coaled, this provided me with a good opportunity to climb up on to the tender to try and straighten it. Some of the lumps must have weighed a couple of hundredweight each, and one such great lump was half on and half off the tender. Somehow I had to make it safe in case it dropped overboard of its own volition on to the track, thus becoming a very serious danger to life and limb. But, try as I might, there was no way of pulling it back inboard. There remained only one option open to me. It would have to go.

I knew that if I didn't pick the opportune moment it would simply roll down the bank and smash the wooden fence to smithereens, but as there was an isolated farmhouse nearby I thought the best thing to do was roll the great lump over the bridge on to the pathway that led into the farm, thus killing two birds with one stone. I would have got rid of the coal and the farmer would have extra fuel for his fire.

As we approached the parapet of the bridge, about thirty seconds away now, I had time to straighten up and look around me in the bright moonlight, and what a deserted desolate spot this was, with the farmhouse situated about two miles up the track off the lonely country road. To avoid hitting the bridge, a few yards short of it I finger-tipped the coal outwards, allowing the slow momentum of the train to slant it at an angle which would allow it to fall plumb into the middle of the pathway below. When it had fallen about half the distance of the 30-foot drop, the engine, now being abreast of the bridge, allowed me a clear view of the pathway I had aimed for.

And there, to my horror, lying in the middle of the pathway were two white naked bodies! They were a young man and woman I would imagine to be in their early twenties. The great black lump of coal, gleaming in the moonlight like a torpedo bomb, hurtled down towards them as straight as an arrow.

They were in my vision for about three seconds, but I was so petrified with fear I could neither utter a word nor move a muscle. I stood there on the tender for another fifteen seconds, believe me, the longest fifteen seconds of my life, horrified by the thoughts flooding through my mind. Suddenly, to my intense relief, I heard the most piercing scream possible. As the train moved slowly on, the screams moved from beneath the bridge out on to the path. Into my sight came running, as though possessed, the figure of a naked woman and she was closely followed by the equally naked figure of the young man shouting at the top of his voice for her to stop while waving both sets of clothing above his head as he ran.

Relief flooded over me at the sight of those two terrified youngsters - I was convinced that I had killed them both. They were still running and screaming when they finally disappeared from my view and merged with the darkness of the night.

On our return journey a few hours later we stopped to look over the side of the bridge. It was daylight by now, and there, scattered around the grass, were the few remaining remnants of clothing. The great lump of coal had buried itself about two feet deep into the soft earth amidst the clothes. It must have been a very close thing indeed and I shudder when I imagine what must have gone through the minds of those two young people as they lay there with a grand slam missile hurtling into the ground only inches from their heads. You could still make out the imprint of their bodies on the grass in the early-morning dew.

Needless to say, I was so terrified of what might have been that I never again took any chances in future years. As far as I was concerned, any coal that had to go over the side in the interests of safety could smash the fences into smithereens - and be damned to the consequences!

15
JUST ANOTHER DAY

Life on the footplate, to the onlooker, must have seemed one long continuation of glamour, thrills and excitement, when in point of fact it was to us merely a job - often a dangerous one, often a boring one, and usually totally devoid of the romance and mystery that the uninitiated picture in their mind.

But the odd day, just the odd one here and there, lives on in my mind. I believe, in retrospect, that as the writer, forty years on, I may perhaps be falling into the same trap as the onlooker.

But am I? I wonder. Has my memory softened, have I forgotten the hard times? The rain and the snow, thick, choking fogs, the back-breaking work, the intense cold of winter, the insufferable heat in high summer? Or am I seeing it in its true light?

Did it all really pass me by, this glamour and excitement and mystery, because it was my job, because I was so intimately involved, because I so desperately needed the money to survive? I don't know the answer - the reader must judge the matter for him or herself. My own mind is too full of conflicting emotions. All I can do is chronicle events as they occurred and hope my memories aren't too confused or clouded.

But yes, in all honesty, I do vividly remember such days, not too many of them, but days that stand out in my mind after half a lifetime. Days of beauty, of contentment. Soft days, kind days, days that will never die while I still retain the ability to just sit and dream and remember the past.

Such a day would begin merely by pushing aside the doors that led into the Loco, a task I had performed countless times over the years and thought no more about it. So why, on this particular morning did things seem different? Why didn't the engines snort and smell of oil and glare menacingly down at me as they usually did? Why was it that on this day the magical smell of heat, oil and steam sent a nostalgic thrill through to my very being?

They weren't snorting, these great engines. They were whispering between themselves, attempting to transfer their thoughts to me. They weren't glaring menacingly down at me, they were smiling - inviting, friendly.

They never tired of their eternal travels. They were ready, they wanted to run. They were asking to be released from the restricting confines of the dark and gloomy Loco, to be free and off out into the fresh air and the sunshine and the far horizons of the open countryside. They wanted to go out for the day, to show themselves off.

They weren't all black and grimy on this day of days, but clean and sparkling. They seemed to vie with one another for my attentions.

'Take me, not Sally on the next bay, or Ruby behind me. Take me, please take me. I've stood here for so long - I've got a good head of steam and I won't let you down. I'll give you a good trip with no trouble. Please, take me!'

Jack, I admonished myself, pull yourself together. They're big, black, ugly engines with no feelings. They don't think and they can't talk - they've no power to transmit coherent thoughts. Or could they? I wonder. You judge - I can't, I'm too involved. Were

they just vehicles of work, the means of earn-
ing a daily crust? Or were they really alive,
feeling and thinking? Did they have good
days and bad ones, just like us mortals? Could
they experience sadness and joy, know the
difference between the two?

No, of course not! But still, I often wonder. . .

'Morning, Jack!' A voice broke into my
thoughts.

I looked up, startled.

'Oh, hello, Charly,' I smiled. Charly West
was my new driver for the year, a nice man, a
quiet man.

'Ready for the off?' he enquired.

'Ready as I'll ever be,' I reflected quietly.
'What engine have we got?'

'She's over there, look,' he pointed. '3637.'

She was one of the Midland Class '3'
freights. In my imagination her 'sisters' in the
loco seemed to retreat into themselves, as
though rejected, whilst 3637 appeared to
sparkle and come alive.

**They never tired of their eternal travels. They were
ready, they just wanted to run. . . Midland 0-6-0 Class
'3F' No 3250.** *Derek Murdoch*

Charly was looking at me, concerned.

'You all right, Jack?'

'Yes, yes, I'm fine thanks.' I had to shake
myself free of the mood I was in, a mood that
seemed to belong to me alone, for Charly
seemed his usual bright cheerful self, anxious
to get on with the day's work.

Our day's work on this day of days was
nothing really out of the ordinary. Just a gentle run through the rolling countryside of
East Nottinghamshire, picking up and setting
down empty and loaded waggons amongst
the small marshalling yards and sidings
between Mansfield and Newark.

We whistled up the signalman at
Mansfield South Junction to allow us out of
the Loco and down the main line to
Mansfield goods yard; one long and two short
whistles was the code for this manoeuvre.
After being turned into the goods yard, Bill
Eric, our guard, announced, 'Not many on
today, Charly. Only twenty wagons. First
stop Mansfield Colliery.'

With a short whistle for the signal we
required, off we set; 3637 seemed to be
straining at the leash, anxious and impatient
to escape the confines of the yard. Charly

gave her just a slight opening of the regulator to stretch the couplings, then out on to the main line we trotted around to Mansfield East Junction where we picked up the single line.

'Morning Charly, morning Jack,' the signalman called as I caught my first tablet. 'Nice day.'

'Yes,' we agreed. 'See you later.'

And it really was a lovely day, I wondered why I hadn't noticed it before.

Up the steep two-mile bank now to Mansfield Colliery, and 3637 took it in her stride. She was loving it. The 'bobby' turned us inside at the junction for our spell of shunting.

'Morning!' he called out as I swapped tablets. 'Beautiful morning.'

I agreed, I had to, for his smiling face deserved such an answer.

Next port of call was Blidworth Junction where a platform had been built many years previously especially for the joint purpose of the 'paddy trains' that fanned out from Mansfield to transport the miners to Rufford and Blidworth collieries, and for when the

'Morning, Jack!' Our first port of call on that glorious spring morning was Mansfield Colliery Junction. *'Blondie' Hurt*

races were being held at Southwell racecourse. I've seen this small country station on many occasions packed to the limit when I crewed passenger trains over this quiet line. We always had one of our Midland Class '4' freights, our 'maids of all work', on these pleasant little diversions.

We pulled into the station to allow our guard to exchange packages and parcels out of his guard's van. There was only the one porter and signalman, no hurry, so we screwed 3637 down and sauntered along to join them. Having finished their chores they were sitting on one of the long platform seats.

'Morning!' they smiled, waving us to a spare seat. 'Cup of tea?' asked the porter. 'I've just brewed up.'

It was, we agreed, a good idea.

We spent a very pleasant half hour in their company. But why were they all smiling, I mused. Were they smiling yesterday? If they were, I must have had my eyes closed.

From Blidworth we now had a lovely stretch of line to traverse, eight miles, all downhill, to Farnsfield. Not much in the way of firing to do, with a light train and only enough steam needed to provide braking power, so I was able to lean out of the cab and watch the world go by.

And what a lovely world it was. The air was still and balmy with the heavy scent of spring flowers growing in profusion on either side of the track pervading your senses. Foxgloves, cowslips, bluebells, penny daisies, all mingling together to add their fragrance to the atmosphere. They really did present a beautiful picture, and all put there by nature. We seemed to be running through rows of glorious blues and whites and yellows with only the twin silver lines to divide them.

New-born lambs were in their element, scampering off to play in the deep lush grass until they realised that they had strayed just a little too far from the protective side of their mothers. Hares and rabbits leapt around in profusion, enjoying their freedom, white cotton-tails bobbing as they chased one another. The air was constantly alive with the hum of honey bees, busy collecting pollen from the mass of flowers all around. Blackbirds, thrushes, sparrows and a family of rooks were all fussily sorting out twigs and straw for their new homes.

In the distance a fox was slinking into the cover of a thick hawthorn hedge, frightened away by our looming presence, his brush quivering in anger at the thought of a lost, easy breakfast.

3637 shook me out of my reverie by blowing off one of her safety valves.

'All right,' I smiled, 'you're telling me that you are too hot on this lovely day - you need cooling down.' I snapped on the injector and she seemed to heave a sigh of relief - 'Ah, that's better!'

We rolled gently into Farnsfield Station and stopped for the familiar exchange of parcels and letters. A new Station Master had been appointed only a fortnight earlier and he could be seen hurrying across the line from the solid, well-maintained station house with its tall distinctive Midland chimneys.

Pretty little Julie, the Farnsfield Station Master's daughter. *Author*

He had his pretty seven-year-old daughter, Julie, with him. She looked delightful in her pink and white frock and straw boater, twin tassels flying behind her as she ran.

'Morning Charly, Morning Jack,' he smiled, looking quite resplendent in his new blue uniform, gold buttons and gold braided cap. 'You're well on time.'

'Can I come up, please?' asked Julie, standing a little nervously beside the giant frame of 3637.

'Yes, of course you can. Don't be afraid, she's as quiet as a mouse now, but mind your pretty frock, don't get it smudged.'

3637 seemed to sense she had a very special guest on her footplate. She behaved impeccably, not a murmur, not a hiss.

I lifted Julie on to my seat where she kicked her legs and clasped her hands, not one bit afraid as she looked up at the quivering needles and highly polished brass wheels and levers. 3637 smiled down on her like the steam-powered Dowager Duchess that she was. Charly gave Julie a sweet - he seemed to have a bottomless pocket for such occasions.

After setting Julie back down on the platform, we set off on the next leg down to

Kirklington, again with a cheery wave from all concerned.

But after we cleared I wondered, again, were they all so cheerful yesterday? Did Julie look so pretty? Was the sun quite so warm, the air so still? And the flowers, were they as beautiful yesterday as they were today? I supposed they were, but if so I hadn't noticed. Even the ploughmen behind their straining teams of Shire horses gave us a wave of recognition.

Only six miles to go, still on a down gradient, with 3637 ambling gently along, at peace with the world, graceful, majestic almost.

The first request from the porter as we drew to a halt was could we top up his coal bunker.

'No problem,' we replied, and set to with a will. Our efforts were rewarded by a gift of a dozen eggs, almost a luxury in those days of acute shortages.

Southwell, with its glorious Minster towering above the roof-tops and chimneys of the sleepy town, was our next destination. We had at least an hour's shunting to do here, for there were still many private small sidings that belonged exclusively to the firms that were situated in and around this part industrial, part farming community. All the shunting was to take place on Charly's side of the engine, so I took myself off to investigate the

famous River Greet, noted for its rainbow trout, or so I had been told even though I never saw any on my previous visits.

Over the fence, across a small field, and I was there. I sat amongst snowdrops and buttercups munching a sandwich. A 'plop' on the surface of the water drew my attention to a spot close by. I looked, and threw in a few crumbs. Yes, they were there - rainbow trout.

I hardly dared to breathe as three of them, magnificently speckled, drifted only a few feet away, their unblinking eyes fascinating me. They appeared to say 'Come on, it's breakfast time. You've had yours.'

I had to agree and threw them the remainder of the bread. Over the next hour I saw no less than a dozen. But why hadn't I seen them before? They must have been there. Perhaps I hadn't looked. Perhaps this day was a bit special to them, too. I shook my head in disbelief. It was as though I'd been re-born. I was seeing things, noticing things I never had before. Had I been going around with my eyes shut, blind and ignorant, just taking things for granted, with the thought in mind that 'what I miss today, I'll see tomorrow.' But if that is your attitude towards life, today is wasted. Yesterday you've almost forgotten, and the indeterminate tomorrow is yet to come. Today is now, it must not be wasted!

To shake myself free of this nonsense I walked across to the opposite edge of the

The Mansfield to Southwell line, fifty years on. As peaceful now as it was then. *Author*

field where I had discovered on another occasion the odd mushroom or two. On arriving there I stopped dead in my tracks, unable to believe my eyes. There was a veritable feast of them. I only cut six, but there was enough in them to provide Charly and myself with garnish for half a dozen breakfasts. I didn't notice them yesterday, I mused. And mushrooms that size must have been at least three or four days old.

But still the penny hadn't dropped. Someone, somewhere, was trying to send me a message. I know now, forty years on, what that message was. 'Jack, for God's sake, don't let this day just slip away. I'm making it a bit special so that it lives on in your mind. It's not a special day, really, it's an ordinary day. But don't you see, everyday's special. You're alive, you're here. Just thank God for it.'

I walked back to the engine lost in thought.

'By gum, Jack,' Charly gasped as he looked at the mushrooms. 'Where on earth did you get those?'

I busied myself building up the engine fire, for now we had a sharp run facing us. It was only ten miles distant to the market town of Newark, but we were now on the busy double-track Nottingham to Lincoln main line and we had to clear it as quickly as possible, as there were many fast trains routed along it and time was of the essence.

We fairly cracked along. Charly gave 3637 her head and she responded magnificently. Click-clack over the points, then dull thunder as we passed over the giant bridge that spanned the River Trent. Whoosh, under a couple of road bridges, then Charly whistled up for the signals that protected the level crossing into Newark. Slam! Off they both flew, stop and distant, clear road ahead now.

The grim, stark outlines of the ruined medieval castle shot into view as 3637 stretched her legs, fairly bounding along. Scree-eech - the wheel flanges resounded as we took the mile-long curve that led us into Newark Station proper. Charly closed the regulator, allowing 3637 to free-wheel and slow down at her own pace.

Past the outer home signal, then the inner, and lastly the home signal appeared through the trees. We whipped by the red and white crossing gates and, this being shopping day, there were crowds of people about, all taking an involuntary step backwards as we thundered through. We carried on past the station, flapping the covers of the books and newspapers on the W. H. Smith bookstall, with the assistant rushing around in a vain attempt to rescue the ones he hadn't weighted down.

The sidings were situated a mile further up the line and the 'bobby' instantly gave us the road to turn inside - there must have been another train on our tail. Sure enough, no sooner had the points closed behind us when the main line stop and distants were pulled off clear.

Five minutes later along came a flyer. A Stanier 'Black 5' hauling a twelve-coach special

At Newark, the shunting and preparation done, there was time to put the billy-can on. A recent view of the station. *Alan Wass*

non-stop to Lincoln whizzed by. 3637 seemed to shrink into insignificance at the sight of her big sister - she knew her place and was respectful.

After an hour's intensive shunting we had marshalled our return train. The next task was to run on to the turntable and spin the engine round for the journey home. Having completed this I climbed up the tender, pulled the coal forward, then topped her up at the water crane to her full capacity of 3,500 gallons. 3637 appeared to appreciate it for, like us, after having been fed and watered she was now ready for anything the world could throw at her.

'Just in time for a mashing, Jack,' said Charly, as he placed the billy-can on the lip of the firebox. In one minute the water was boiling, in went the tea and sugar and we sat back to enjoy our brew.

'You know something, Jack,' Charly chuckled, 'I wouldn't change places with the King right now.'

By this time we'd unpacked our bread and cheese sandwiches, peeled an onion apiece and broken out the salt.

'By gum,' he went on, 'this is the life. I don't know why it is but tea never tastes so good anywhere else as when it's brewed over the engine fire.'

After we'd eaten, Charly asked, 'Do you want to take her back, Jack? I'll do the firing.'

This was all too rare a change for me, so I readily agreed. The reason I'd spent so long on the shovel was due purely to the fact that the great majority of drivers with whom I had been booked over the years had been too old for any real hard graft. In all honesty, they'd done their share, but Charly, still being only forty, relished a spell of firing.

At 2.30 I whistled up for the signals that turned us out main line. No luck yet - instead the signals dropped for a through passenger train to Nottingham.

However, five minutes later off they came and we began our return journey, which was to be a repeat, in reverse order, of our outward run. Once clear of the sidings and station I gave 3637 half regulator and notched her up on the valve gear twenty per cent. She fairly flew along - she was

preening herself, and I could almost hear her saying 'Hmm, "Black 5s" aren't all that much better than I am. They can give them fancy names if they like, but I'd already covered a million miles before they were even born!'

Our return journey was different, but only if you took the time to notice. The lambs, tired after their morning's frolic, were having a little siesta by the side of their mothers. The rabbits had all disappeared into the coolness and safety of their burrows, and the birds were enjoying a well-earned rest after their home-building stint. Fields had been ploughed, the pungent smell of freshly turned earth heavy to the nostrils.

The air was not quite so fragrant as the spring flowers closed their petals to protect themselves from the withering heat. The human population was also a bit thin on the ground after the morning's work, and even old 3637 seemed to be flagging somewhat as we topped the rise before dropping down into Mansfield goods yard.

Well, I mused, she must be thirty years old if she's a day. But she'd enjoyed her day out, I was sure of that. Her old plates were creaking a bit, but she was still game.

And I'd enjoyed my day out. I'm convinced I returned a different man from the one that had set out. Yet how could I be? I was only eight hours older, and apart from being a little more introspective than usual, I was the same man, the same me. There were no visible differences that the world at large would notice, and I was absolutely certain that when I woke the following morning I would look upon today as just another yesterday. Or would I?

As we ran old 3637 over the ash-pit in the Loco to have her fire cleaned in readiness for tomorrow, wherever they might take her, I could have sworn she gave a long sigh of relief. She too was tired, but I'll bet she was happy.

Charly turned to me as we left the loco and, placing a friendly arm around my shoulder he asked, 'Sure you're alright, Jack? You've been very quiet.'

'Yes,' I answered. 'I must have had a mood on me. I'll be alright tomorrow.'

16
FULL STEAM AHEAD

At about the period 1950-51, the railways, having by this time recovered from the ravages of war, had replaced engines, rolling-stock and, where necessary, lines. They also started to try and bring back a little colour and pleasure into the lives of people by re-introducing the excursion trips that had proved so popular before the war. As these were in the main long-distance express trains, they invariably picked crews that were used to passenger work and, as I came into this category, I was fortunate enough to be included on more than my fair share of them.

I did several middle-distance runs to Skegness and the popular Derbyshire towns of Matlock and Buxton. Then, as luck would have it, I was chosen to do a couple of Blackpool trips. On the first of these I was teamed up with a driver I knew very well, having worked with him before on many occasions.

His name was Eric Swain, only five or six years older than myself. We used to fight to get these jobs, for not only were they a pleas-ant change from our normal, repetitive work-ing day, but also we would clear about three days' pay into the bargain. Although we were relieved by a set of Blackpool men as soon as we ran in, we were considered to be on con-tinuous duty, therefore we were paid accord-ingly. As my wages were still only £10 a week, and we were struggling to bring up the two children, the extra money was used to provide us with a few extra comforts in life, such as sweets for the children, and to be able to go out for a drink or to the pictures - commonplace today, but still very much a rarity for most people in those far off days.

We had been allocated one of the big Stanier 'Black 5s', No 4845, for this run. We were due to run the empty coaches down to Whitwell, then pick up passengers at all sta-tions to Pye Bridge. From there we were non-stop to Longsight, Manchester, where we had to pick up another driver who had signed for the road through to Blackpool, as my mate had only signed for as far as Manchester.

I have often thought when reading about the arduous task that faced the fireman on these large coal-hungry steam engines, that his role was overshadowed by the role of the driver. If you stop to consider a moment, the driver's part of the operation consisted of sit-ting on his seat and making the odd adjust-ment to either the regulator, reversing lever or brake. Added to this, of course, was the fact that he knew the road, which was second nature to him anyway having probably trav-elled over the same stretch of line many hun-dreds of times.

Compare this with the life of the fireman who, for literally hours on end, had so much to do that even stopping to have a mug of tea was very often out of the question. Not always, of course, but whenever the engine was being worked heavy you just didn't have time to breathe, or so it seemed. It's no won-der that whenever we had the opportunity to do a day's driving we leapt at the chance. It was as good as a day off!

The route took us through the beautiful Derbyshire countryside via Ambergate and Matlock, then up and over the heavy bank with its many tunnels and steeply banked curves through Peak Forest and the Goyt Valley. There the line started to drop down

We were allocated Stanier 'Black 5' No 44845 for my first excursion trip over the Pennines to Manchester and on to Blackpool. *J. F. Henton*

the opposite side of the hills into Manchester, where we stopped to fill up with water; we would have used about 2,000 gallons blasting our way over the Pennines. At this point we also picked up our spare driver. This made life a little easier for me as Eric then started to take turns with me in firing. This was no mean task with a firebox five feet wide and twelve feet in length, and the way the Manchester driver was tearing along meant that we were firing continuously.

Our route next took us through Preston, then on to the long level straight into Blackpool where the happy colourful throng of passengers spilled out on to the platform to savour the many attractions of this popular North West seaside resort.

We were relieved the moment we ran in,

The view from the guard's brake of a Blackpool excursion looking towards the sharp end, approaching Chinley, near Manchester. *Ray Dakin*

so made our way into the loco messroom for a wash and brush up, then, discarding our overalls, went out to join forces with the thousands of holiday-makers. Quite naturally, our first port of call was the nearest pub for a few well-deserved pints. On from there for a fish and chip dinner, then, with our Manchester driver acting as guide, for this was home ground to him, a tour of the high spots.

As this was my first trip here it was all new and exciting. We weren't due to sign on again until eight o'clock at night, which afforded us the opportunity to have another meal and a few more pints to set us up for the long haul back.

Having changed back into working gear, we climbed back on to the footplate to have a quick check round before coming off the shed to back on to our twelve-coach train in the platform. The Blackpool men had cleaned the fire, filled her up to her capacity of 4,500 gallons, and with around eight tons of bright steam coal, well trimmed and stacked, we were all set.

I built up the fire steadily until I had a white-hot box full, and with ten minutes to go and the passengers beginning to stream on to the platform in a noisy but good-natured way, I was as ready for the hard slog as I ever would be.

One of the passengers, a jovial, good-natured man, asked if he could come up on to the footplate, and as there were no bowler-hatted men in the vicinity at this time of night, we said OK. He brought up a question which, until that time, had never even crossed my mind: 'Whenever a group of people are taken on an outing by coach, someone, at the end of the day, will always organise a collection for the driver. But in my experience, this never happens on a train. Why?'

We, of course, agreed, and he then promised to see what he could do for us. True to his word, when we eventually arrived back in Mansfield he handed us a straw hat full of assorted coins which amounted to £5 when we counted it. We duly thanked him for his initiative and his efforts on our behalf, then split it three ways between the guard, Eric and myself. To the best of my knowledge, this was the one and only time this ever happened in all my fifteen years on the footplate.

As the events of the night began to unfold, I didn't do too badly at all. Eric volunteered to fire the engine back as far as Manchester, so I immediately climbed aboard the first coach at the rear of our 'Black 5' and was instantly plied with cakes, sandwiches and bottles of beer. So much so that by the time we reached Longsight where our spare driver was to leave us, I was ready for anything.

I climbed up on to the tender and pulled the water crane across to top us up. This was our last chance to fill up before reaching home, still a long way off yet for we had the bank up and over the Pennines facing us and we would be working heavily.

With a white-hot fire illuminating the night sky and blowing off steam through both safety valves, off we set at a cracking pace and fairly stormed our way through the one and three-quarter miles of Dove Holes tunnel to the summit. There was a 60 miles per hour limit down the other side due to the tightly banked curves, but I swear we must have been doing 70 at times with the engine running freely downhill.

These Staniers could certainly steam, so much so that this was the one and only occasion during my life on the footplate that I got the wind up. We were literally being thrown all over the place. Every time we hit a curve the banking would tilt the engine over at an angle and tend to throw us outwards. Then immediately the reverse would happen on the opposite side. I'd had enough of this so I sprung open the tender doors and started cracking coal up to take my mind off the violent see-saw effect of the engine. I was damned glad to run into Ambergate at the bottom and approach some semblance of normality. I had managed somehow to get a good fire on for the next leg of the journey, which was a ten-mile up-hill stretch to Pye Bridge, up which we absolutely stormed with fire blasting out of the chimney in an unending stream.

We had been 15 minutes late out of Manchester, but we arrived in Mansfield, finally home, ten minutes early. I don't honestly think I've ever travelled so fast on an engine before in my life!

Altogether it was a smashing day out, but boy, was I tired! We had signed on at six the previous morning, and signed off 21 hours later at three o'clock on Monday morning. We'd burned 14 tons of coal and used 12,000 gallons of water in the process. What a day!

My next Blackpool trip, a month later, was a very different and in many respects more enjoyable excursion. Instead of picking up passengers *en route*, the whole train was fully booked by a working men's club from Mansfield.

For this trip we had been allocated one of the 2-6-0 'Crabs', No 42774, a much older engine built during the '30s but incorporating many of the modern improvements that were to be found on more recent engines - innovations such as left-hand drive, a spacious cab, and more comfortable seats for the fireman and driver. The boilers were only pressed at 180 lbs per square inch instead of the more normal 225 lbs, but the important thing was that she steamed very well. You only had to show her the shovel and the safety valves would begin to pop.

As we backed onto the twelve-coach train we noticed, much to our delight, that the first coach next to the engine was where they stored the beer and provisions; being a club they had provided their own refreshments.

Owing to pressure of traffic in the Preston and Manchester area, we had been given a different route. We were booked to travel over the Seymour Bank, picking up the main line to Leeds at Foxloe Junction, then on to Cudworth, Sowerby Bridge, Bury, Blackburn and Rose Grove, a very round about route.

My driver was Fred Parker, a smashing man only a few years older than myself. We literally flew over the bank, quite unlike the heavy coal trains we were used to hauling over that line with a banker. Our first stop was for water at Woodhouse Mill, and as I climbed over the tender the steward in charge of the drinks leaned out and passed up

A typical holiday excursion train - the 'City of Nottingham Holiday Express'. *Nottingham Evening Post*

A typical scene of eager crowds waiting for a special excursion train. *Nottingham Evening Post*

to me two quart bottles of Mansfield Golden Drop, a favourite bitter in those days. From then on, each time we stopped to fill up this procedure was repeated. I've never stopped at so many water cranes in my life. By the time we reached Blackpool we finished up with a locker full of empty bottles!

We picked up our first new driver at Cudworth, my mate only having signed for the road to this point. Our second driver joined at Sowerby Bridge, and our third at Rose Grove. We eventually finished up at Blackpool with four drivers and one fireman in the cab, such was the meandering route we had been forced to follow.

The last driver that we had picked up at Rose Grove was a short figure of a man and, true to type, he was the heaviest of them all

as far as working the engine was concerned. This was one of those paradoxes - the shorter the driver, the heavier they were with the controls. You could have a six-foot-plus man weighing all of sixteen stone and he would coax and caress the engine carefully and gently along. Put any little bloke in the driving seat and his first inclination would be to blast away. This fellow was no exception - we fairly flew along the last fifty miles into Blackpool.

When we did run in, the procedure was much the same as before. We were immediately relieved by a set of Blackpool men and off we went, all five of us, down to the nearest pub.

The return journey was a reversal of the outward run, dropping off our conductors *en*

All signals showing clear for Blackpool - our 2-6-0 'Crab', No 42774. *Ray Dakin*

route until there was only Fred and me on the footplate. As on our outward journey, every time we stopped at a water crane, out would pop the steward with two quarts of beer. I don't believe I've ever drunk so much in a 24-hour period, before or since, but somehow I never got drunk.

I finished up in Mansfield firing in my socks - my boots were just too damned heavy to keep lifting them off the floor!

EPILOGUE

During the year of 1954 I had the opportunity of going into business on my own account, a chance too good to miss. But such was the pull and calling of life on the footplate as a lifelong career, that my workmates just couldn't take it seriously that I would leave. You never left the footplate until you were carried off.

I handed in my notice to a Mr Tarlin, our chief clerk, and three times he gave it back to me telling me not to be so foolish and to go home and talk things over with my father.

Eventually, however, my notice was accepted, and I did my last firing turn on a steam engine.

As I left the Loco for the last time I looked around at all those beautiful gleaming monsters with their own unique smell of steam and oil which can be found nowhere else in

Even by the early 1950s the railway I had been brought up on was changing, and soon scenes such as this became commonplace. Another magnificent engine is dismantled at Bulwell Forest. *Nottingham Evening Post*

the world other than in a steam locomotive shed. And I must admit that tears sprang to my eyes as I remembered all the marvellous characters I had known and the memorable trips I had made in their company with these fine engines that stood there looking down at me.

I thought of old Charlie Jones and the fun we had together. Of Tommy West with his impromptu and somewhat scary outbursts of hymn singing. Of my old mate Alf Botham and our trips on pay-day down to the Midland Station Hotel with his dog, Sally, where we would have our pint of bitter and she her mild; and how she would always be the first to finish her tipple before we even started ours - and of many, many more. Characters who had come into my life, striding through it and shaping it and enriching it beyond belief.

A quiet sadness crept over me as I realised that these times were gone forever, never to return. Not only had many of these remarkable characters died, but the whole structure and life of the railways was changing with the gradual phasing out of our beloved steam engines to make way for the faceless and characterless diesels and electrics. The railways and the life I had been brought up with were disappearing rapidly.

One of my closest railwaymen friends, Walt Haynes, who is still employed on the railway and is by this time a long-serving driver, keeps me up to date with all the latest railway gossip. We often have long conversations regarding the merits and de-merits of steam engines versus diesels, but on one subject we agree wholeheartedly. Whilst on diesels you have all the refinements such as fully enclosed and heated cabs, armchair-type seats, a hotplate to keep your tea warm, even a point in which to plug your kettle or frying-pan to cook bacon and eggs, there is not the comradeship that existed between driver and fireman.

On diesels, apart from the express trains, there is only one man and, as Walt graphically describes his job as he sees it, 'You are nothing but a glorified tram driver!'

In many ways it is certainly a much safer and more comfortable way of life now. All the trains, even coal trains, are close coupled and fitted with a continuous brake throughout; you therefore have none of the problems that were inherent in the loose-coupled trains, such as possibly breaking the train in two, or that real nightmare that we all had to live with, the runaway.

But, on the other hand, in my day you felt a tremendous sense of satisfaction after completing a hard day's work, pitting your strength and skill against a steam engine that refused to steam properly. Or literally fighting your way up and over a steep bank where you had to pull out all the stops using all the knowledge you had acquired over many years just to keep going, trying your damnedest to make certain the engine didn't beat you - or break you. You would then look back at the end of your shift with a sense of pride and achievement, making your way home tired out and drained, but you'd have a feeling of exhilaration that is totally without parallel on the railways of today.

Now, many years later, whenever Maisie and I have a run out in the car and are anywhere within the vicinity of one of our old LMS lines or stations, I never fail to make a detour to stop and have a look round.

Memories always come flooding back to me. Where there was once vibrant life and colour and noise, all I see now are the wild flowers springing up where the twin silver line used to be. They are everywhere, growing up through the cracks in the platform where once people like little Julie used to stand and wave us off. Just a haven now for the birds and other wildlife.

As I close my eyes, sounds begin to break the silence of a past long forgotten, and memories of many years are condensed into minutes as I lean out over my cab door. Platforms are crowded with people off on their journeys, carefree children off to the seaside for the day, watched over by proud mothers in new dresses, and protective fathers looking decidedly uncomfortable in Sunday suits. Husbands and wives, lovers, all holding hands until the very last moment before the slowly moving train rends them tearfully apart; soldiers off to the war, for many, the last farewell, sailors returning,

Above A scene of desolation, but not devoid of memories of busier, more colourful times. Those smoke-blackened arches have many stories to tell! *Peter Brown*

Below Thorneywood Station in the Nottingham outskirts, closed in 1951. One of thousands of such places gone for ever. *Nottingham Evening Post*

Keeping my hand in. On the footplate of a passenger tankie at the Midland Railway Centre, Butterley, 1986. *Author*

Not quite so innocent now (see page 56)! Myself and my wife Maisie fifty years on, August 1991. *Author*

porters milling about with their carts, the Station Master going about his day's work, and little Julie, still waving.

How can anyone say that this sad, forlorn and deserted station is empty, lifeless? No, it is full to overflowing with untold years of memories and ghosts.

I know it may sound silly to expect things to be the same as they were thirty-five years ago, but every time I step on to a line or station I am looking and listening for the sound and the sight of one of our old steam engines to come blasting through, with a shout and a cheer from one of my old friends. I am always disappointed. The days of Blaster Bowen are gone forever.

None the less, the tremendous attraction that steam railways still hold for today's population, whether they be lads, dads or granddads, doesn't surprise me in the least. The age of the great steam engines had a tremendous impact on everyone's lives, so profound that I honestly believe it will live on forever.

Whenever you visit one of the many railway museums or one of the privately owned steam railways, you will discover a throng of people eager to learn everything they can about the hot, smelly, noisy monsters they see before them. I have been fortunate enough to have many a ride on the footplate since leaving the railway, for we often take Kirsten and Holly, our two granddaughters, to local preserved railways. As soon as I tell the driver I've had fifteen years firing on them, he invariably invites us up on to the footplate. The two girls, of course, love this. It's a completely different world from the one they've grown up in, and they are the envy of all the other children on the platform.

When I stand back and watch the thousands of people milling around the engines I cannot help but think what old Charlie Jones would have made of all this enthusiasm. I think me and Charlie, as a team, would have made enough cigarettes out of that lot to last us a whole year!

But there I go, dreaming again. I wonder if I will ever come to my senses.

God - I sincerely hope not.

INDEX